How to be yo

How to be your own boss
Conrad Frost

© Conrad Frost 1979, 1981

All rights reserved. No part of this publication may be reproduced or transmitted, in any form or by any means, without permission

First edition published 1979 by Arthur Barker Ltd

Second edition published in Papermac 1981 by
THE MACMILLAN PRESS LTD
London and Basingstoke
Companies and representatives
throughout the world

ISBN 0 333 30012 2

Printed in Hong Kong

The paperback edition of this book is sold subject to the condition that it shall not, by way of trade or otherwise, be lent, resold, hired out, or otherwise circulated without the publisher's prior consent, in any form of binding or cover other than that in which it is published and without a similar condition including this condition being imposed on the subsequent purchaser

Contents

Introduction	vii
1: Nobody ever became a millionaire on a salary	1
2: Forming and registering businesses	22
3: Capital, finance and funding	33
4: Income Tax	50
5: Keeping books, records and accounts	73
6: VAT	85
7: National Insurance	106
8: Self-employment pensions and insurance	118
9: Licences	135
10: Becoming a shopkeeper	148
11: Where to get help	169
Index	179

Grateful acknowledgement is given for the professional advice and assistance of, in alphabetical order:

Alan Carswell,
John Cooper,
Phillip Lewis
and my wife, Brandi, whose role is more fully explained on pages 68 and 69 of this book.

Introduction

Anyone glancing at this book in a shop and proposing to buy it in order to enjoy the advantages of self-employment should ensure that a proper receipt is obtained from the bookseller. The book will then already have begun to serve its purposes of informing and advising to profitable advantage for, in these circumstances and with its use in business established, its cost will become a tax-deductible expense. And one of the first lessons for anyone going into business on his own account is that one should never miss a discount, even if it is called something else.

This book sets out to be not only an introductory guide and a comprehensive source of information to anyone about to embark upon any aspect of self-employment but to remain thereafter the *only* book of general reference that will ever be needed. It is specifically compiled for the use of people commencing part-time gainful work, people commencing businesses as sole traders, setting up partnership businesses, acquiring existing businesses, and forming or acquiring limited liability companies. It is intended to be a book that will become dog-eared by constant use.

The presentation of the material in such a book is dictated by the fact that it is written for many different readers – and each reader's problems will be individual. The first chapter is designed to enable the individual reader to identify himself or herself and, with the help of the subsequent chapter headings and the index, to refer quickly to all personally relevant material. Where specific information relates to more than one main aspect of the subject it is repeated wherever relevant, in whatever detail is in context with its particular reference.

The claim that no other book on the subject will ever be needed by the reader needs qualification. It assumes that the services and advice of a bank manager, solicitor, accountant and other professional advisors are used where these are recommended. At the same time it is recognized that these services are not obligatory. What these professional services do, and how they do it, is described for the benefit of the reader who decides to undertake any particular part of the administration of his business venture without professional help.

In this connection there arises the problem of making references to specific professional services – other than those of bank manager, solicitor and accountant. The simple way out would be to put a professionally accepted classification upon a service being recommended, and to direct the reader to the local telephone directory or *Yellow Pages* for listings under the classification. However, in some areas of the United Kingdom there are services which do not have listed entries – under any acceptable or recognizable category – in either telephone directory or *Yellow Pages*. This book therefore gives the name, address and telephone number of a specialist professional service, where the use of such a service is referred to, in the text; lists of additional addresses are in the last chapter. Wherever possible these references have been based on satisfactory personal experience or investigation, but they do not necessarily constitute a recommendation based upon the author's personal experience.

1: Nobody ever became a millionaire on a salary

A recent Department of Employment estimate showed that nearly two million people in the United Kingdom are in self-employment, earning livings for themselves and their dependants. They include doctors and dentists, plumbers and piano tuners, window cleaners and writers, typists and taxi drivers – and the tens of thousands of people who run a 'corner shop'. They include the millionaire who publishes newspapers and the newsagent who sells them.

Some, like the doctors and dentists, must be qualified to practise. Others, like the taxi drivers, have to obtain specific licences to operate their businesses. All are subject to special categories of taxation and all must observe regulations of various kinds, both national and local, relating to self-employment. Nevertheless, in the United Kingdom, anyone who wishes to do so may set up in business and become his or her own boss.

Those who take this step may or may not need capital. They may or may not need special skills or relevant experience. But some things they must have in common. They must have courage. They must have an ability to work harder, longer and probably for less reward than would be assured in a wage-earning or salaried job.

Nobody ever became a millionaire on a salary. This fact has possibly been what has inspired many people to go into business on their own account. On the other hand the majority of self-employed people never expect and never get much more than a living from their businesses. The real rewards – and this is true for all the self-employed – are independence and the knowledge that the results of hard work, or of good ideas, do not have to be shared with others who did not do the work, or who did not have the ideas.

Each of those joining the ranks of the self-employed – those for whom this book has been written – belongs to one or another of a number of different main categories. These are now briefly described and commented upon so that the individual reader may be able to make a self-identification and then the more easily recognize, in subsequent chapters of the book, information relevant to himself or herself – and to his or her potential future.

MEN AND WOMEN
Despite discriminatory attitudes and legislation, even in 1971 one-fifth of all the self-employed were women. The most recent Department of Employment analysis of the self-employed shows that women are competitive with men in almost every main area of industry except those linked with heavy mechanical engineering, construction work and transport.

Legislation cannot create an equality which is neither physically inherent nor generally desired by men and women in their relationship with one another. The main areas of self-employment opportunities for women therefore are likely to remain in textiles, leather and fur goods, clothing, publishing, the distributive trades, business services and those other special services, like midwifery, modelling and cosmetic demonstration, which for one obvious reason or another will always be categorized by sex. Because of domestic responsibilities, part-time, home-based self-employment involves a higher percentage of the self-employed women than of the self-employed men.

Having recognized the ratio of women to men in self-employment, and having remarked upon its pattern, for convenience this book will not again refer separately to women except where there is a specific reason for doing so.

AGE GROUPINGS

The age at which people go into business on their own account is usually directly linked with the reason for taking the step. It often also dictates the nature of the business and may be predictive of the prospects of success.

At one extreme of a time scale there are two categories of young people who, on the threshold of becoming self-employed, have no decisions to make and no doubts to resolve. They have never considered any alternative to self-employment. Their prospects of success are high.

One of these groups is that of the young people whose education and training has been of a specialized nature, qualifying or preparing them for professions which generally, if not exclusively, are practised by the self-employed. These are the young people preparing, for example, for the medical profession, or training with an organization like RADA for a theatrical profession. They may include some who, like the junior hospital 'houseman', may regard an initial period of salaried employment as a final 'apprenticeship' stage of training. The other group is of those whose gainful occupation has been decided by considerations of inheritance. They were 'born into' a family business.

People in both these categories, because of their training, apprenticeship or their gradual familiarization with the family business, are likely to know the regulations and to be aware of the special problems relating to their particular kind of businesses. Certainly those being carefully guided into small, established family businesses, which will one day be theirs, are unlikely to need this or any other book on self-employment.

It can be a very different situation at the other end of the time scale. Here are the older people who have completed one working life as employees and who, upon reaching pensionable age, have decided either to supplement their pensions by gainful self-employment – or who may even be inspired by the fact that it is 'never too late to make a million'. Here are many fit, active people who are sensitive about the description of senior citizen and who find it impossible to regard themselves as elderly. They have been at least moderately successful or possibly highly successful in employment; now they have perhaps limited self-employment ambitions matched by limited capital. Savings, annuities, matured endowment policies, the commuted part of a company pension – all these may be thrown at risk. Yet this is the category of the self-employed most vulnerable to disappointments, losses and failures, and the one with the least hope of recovery to try again.

Any reader in this category should be very self-critical, very realistic and exceedingly cautious before committing himself to the undoubted hazards of going into business. The reasons why they did not go into business on their own account earlier may now weigh heavily against many people in this category. There is no business so small that it does not demand ambition, drive and self-confidence if it is to survive, let alone succeed. If it was a lack of these qualities that prevented the pensioner from 'going it alone' when younger, then those qualities are not going to develop now. And if the considerations that weighed in favour of spending the normal working life-time as a wage-earning or salaried employee were the advantages of a job which offered paid holidays, sick pay, subsidized canteen facilities, union-negotiated protection, security and income increases, then pensionable age is usually far too late for a personal confrontation with the stern realities of competitive business.

Generally, however, anyone reaching pensionable age who proposes to go into business on his or her own account will not have done so earlier because the work they did as an employee was not of a nature that allowed them to use their trained skill or their acquired experience in a business venture of their own. The process engraver in a newspaper office, the air traffic controller and the worker on an automobile assembly line, for example, cannot set up in business on their own account doing the one job they know and are good at.

The majority of people seeking self-employment after reaching pensionable age have to look for a completely new kind of business. Whatever they choose, usually they know little or nothing about it. It is too late in life for them, and far too speculative, to launch a completely new business of a kind in which they have no experience. They need something 'ready-made' and shown to be producing enough income to justify the investment.

Often the small shop, with living accommodation, seems the complete answer to their needs. Many such people acquire ready-made businesses of this kind without a proper appreciation of the problems and without getting the advice they should have – and which is available. The reader recognizing himself to be in this category will find that Chapter 10 deals with the practical issues involved.

In between the two described extremes of youth and age lie the majority of those joining the ranks of the self-employed – employees proposing to take either the first step or a full stride from dependence upon a wage or salary to financial independence. Among *their* numbers are the next-generation millionaires !

Those taking the first step of spare-time work may have no intention at the time – or ever have the intention – of doing more than supplement wage or salary. Their sole intention may even be simply to have a sense of independence, so that they may 'thumb their nose' at either employer or union if they want to. Their intention may be merely to avoid having 'all their eggs in one basket', and to know that they would survive, meet their personal commitments and maintain a reasonable standard of living if the paid employment came to a sudden end. Or they may be consciously striving to establish a foundation for a planned full-time business, either upon retirement or earlier.

The 'full stride' group contains a hard core of those who had always planned to take the step when they were ready, or when the opportunity arose, and they will generally have learnt their business by having been employed in it – often in a deliberately chosen range and diversity of jobs within the same business. A good example is the restaurateur who has already familiarized himself or herself in employment with every aspect of restaurant work, from chef and waiter to maître d'hôtel. Such people are the most certain survivors because they know exactly what they are doing.

Others will be taking the plunge because they have recognized a fortuitous opportunity and because it is in their natures to have the courage and self-confidence to take a chance if the odds are good. These are the people most likely to end up with personalized number plates on their Rolls Royces!

Others will be the victims of redundancies, with capital suddenly made available from statutory compensatory payments. They may see their misfortune as a welcome opportunity to have a crack at being their own boss – at somebody else's expense. Or they may recognize little hope of re-employment and may prefer the independence of self-employment to a dependency upon Social Security benefits. They are a comparatively new phenomenon in the business world.

For others the opportunity may have been provided by a legacy or some other financial windfall. But picking the right eight drawn games on a football pool coupon or holding a top-prize-winning Premium Bond endows nobody with business acumen. And it requires none to recognize that a £250,000 windfall invested in local authority bonds, currently obtaining $11\frac{1}{2}\%$, will produce an income of £28,750 before tax. The desire to go into business and the necessity to do so should never be confused. It is a chilling fact of life that nobody loses money faster in business ventures than those who won it in the first place.

HOME, OFFICE OR FACTORY?
One of the most important categorizations of the self-employed is that based upon the place of work. Most of the regulations that the self-employed have a responsibility to comply with, and most of the licences, certificates and permits they may have to obtain, are related to the place of work. So are some of the considerable Income Tax business expenses they may

succeed in claiming. These matters are dealt with in detail in later chapters. Here it is sufficient to point out that broadly speaking the self-employed differ from the employed in that their businesses are often home-based, and that almost all part-time self-employment is home-based.

The term 'home-based' is used because it covers several types of business from a tax point of view. Nor should a confusion arise about 'home work', where an employee does work for an employer who does not provide a place of business. People doing work of this kind at home are not self-employed.

For the self-employed the first kind of 'home-based' work is that in which the actual work is done in the home without any particular room or area being specifically allocated for business purposes. The typical example is that of the home typist who may use the dining-room table for three or four afternoons' work during an average week. There is an important difference between this use of the home as a place of business and the use in which, necessarily, an area or room in the home is specifically used or equipped for the purposes of the business. The freelance photographer, for instance, will need the facilities of a professionally equipped and temperature-controlled dark-room.

Although questions of tax are dealt with in Chapter 4, the significance of the difference between the two cases above has to be explained here. The typist would find it difficult to persuade the Inland Revenue that some part of her rent, rates, heating and lighting bills should be allowed as business expenses. It would be reasonably argued that these expenses would have been incurred anyway, and that they had not increased as a consequence of her work.

The freelance photographer would have a much better case although it would be strengthened if his business had commenced during the tax year in which he had moved into the house. On the other hand, if he established the claim for his dark-room as being used exclusively for his business – so that allowance was made for light, heat and a proportion of rates –

he would later lose part of his capital gains exemption on a private residence if he came to sell the property.

The best of both worlds is possible if it can be established that some part of the home is used essentially for business purposes, but not exclusively so.

The third category of home-based business exists in the case of professional people like doctors and dentists who must set aside a surgery, a waiting-room and possibly toilet facilities because the general public come to the private residence where a professional service is being provided. Where a partnership of this kind is operating from the senior partner's home and when receptionists, nurses and a secretary are employed, the business use of the premises may take precedence over the residential use.

The fourth category of home-based business goes one step further because here the living accommodation goes with the job. The most obvious examples are the farmer with his farmhouse and the small shopkeeper with living premises behind and above his shop. In such cases the location and nature of the home is determined by and is subordinate to the needs of the business.

The final category of home-based businesses is the one that explains the real necessity for the term. These are the self-employed who work *from* home but not – except for the 'paper work' – *at* home. The window cleaner, gardener, decorator and the freelance sales representative are examples within the grouping.

Limited Liability companies may be run from the home, which may be registered as the business address. Staff may be employed in a business being run from the home. Few part-time businesses operate from offices, industrial manufacturing factories or similar premises. But part-time business ventures that succeed usually develop into full-time businesses. It is when these succeed that the business often outgrows the home, that a limited liability company may be formed, that staff may be employed and that business premises of one kind or another may become required. It is at this point that the self-employed become the most deeply involved in the observation of regulations of all kinds – those relating to employment and to business premises in particular.

TYPES OF BUSINESS
Since every employer is himself or herself self-employed there is no aspect of business that lies outside the scope of this examination. Many people intending to become self-employed already have skills, training or experience that decide the kind of business they will go into. If you are an employee hair stylist who has decided to go into business on your own account because you have realized that you are the assistant most asked for by clients, you will open a hairdressing salon of your own, not a greengrocery.

Those who do not have special skills, training or experience and who have to choose a field of business to enter, need first to realize that all businesses fall into one or another of four classifications, each having aspects of suitability or unsuitability for the inexperienced. The four categories are:
1. Manufacturing businesses
2. Production businesses
3. Trading businesses
4. Service businesses.

1. Manufacturing businesses These are businesses in which, with the use of equipment and labour, raw or basic materials are converted by a manufacturing process, usually in quantity, into consumer goods for sale, either to the general public or to a trade market. Sales to the general public are normally made through the medium of trading businesses.

This kind of industry normally requires special premises which may have to satisfy local zoning regulations for either light or heavy industry. The manufacturing process may, anyway, create noise or other environmental pollution which would rule out a home-based operation. Manufacturing equipment usually represents high initial investment. Production on a quantitative scale to justify the investment usually involves the employment of a labour force.

All these factors weigh against manufacturing businesses as a choice for either spare-time or full-time self-employment for the inexperienced. Certainly they normally rule out the home-based business.

However, no generalization is ever wholly true. There are notable exceptions, mostly in the field of handicraft products – for example pottery, jewellery and leather work.

2. **Production businesses** These are involved in growing or breeding. The produce or the product is either sold to a manufacturing business as raw material or, through the medium of a trading business, to the public. Some aspects of the production business do have direct sales contact with the public – for example, the dog breeder.

Again, apart from a few exceptions like domestic animal breeding and – on the growing side – mushroom cultivation, production businesses are not generally suitable for part-time self-employment. They generally need round-the-clock, week in week out availability throughout the year. Indeed people in these businesses generally have to 'live in' with the job.

This does not make a production business necessarily suitable to start up from the home, however. It is the other way round. Usually a home suitable for the business is needed to form the essential link, typified by the farm and its farmhouse. One may run a successful part-time or even full-time typing agency from a high-rise flat in a city centre, but a bee-keeping business would mean a move out into the country.

3. **Trading businesses** These buy the goods made by a manufacturing business, or the produce grown by a producer, and sell them at profit to other people – generally, but not necessarily, to the public.

As a rule this is a category of business which requires special premises where the goods or produce may be stocked, displayed for inspection and sold – in other words a shop, stall or warehouse. Since the profit on what is sold has to be kept competitively low, success depends on the biggest possible turnover of the goods or produce and this in turn means carrying plenty of stock. The investment in stock – or the outstanding debt for stock bought on short-term credit in the hope that it will have been sold at profit before it has to be paid for – together with the need for special premises both to store and display goods – generally rules out trading businesses as being suitable for part-time self-employment or for home-based work.

Again there are exceptions. The small shop very often offers a home as well as a business – but with the attendant risk that if the business fails then the home is lost too. Such businesses are not, of course, suitable for part-time self-employment.

On the other hand import-export agents and mail-order agents do not usually handle the goods in which they deal. Such businesses, until and unless they develop into large-scale operations, are ideal for operation from the home. The small-scale, mail-order agencies, indeed, represent a well-known source of pin-money to housewives, although this kind of work, with its obvious limitations on development, cannot really be defined as a business and is not what this book is about.

There are always special exceptions to every rule. Where the commodity being traded in is small and valuable, and when the self-employed trader knows his business and has his contacts, very profitable home-based, spare-time or full-time businesses may be developed. Dealers trading in gold, silver, diamonds and other precious stones are examples of traders who may operate with great success from a home base.

4. Service businesses It is in this fourth and final business classification that most part-time self-employment lies. And in those services that require full-time involvement, this is still the group of businesses that has the attraction of being generally the most suitable for a home-based operation.

Service businesses usually require little or no stock. They may need little special equipment and the initial outlay may be negligible. Any equipment that may be required does not usually create problems of storage, accommodation space, noise or other neighbour disturbance.

A part-time or full-time service business may be operated *at* home – for example, freelance writing, art work or any similar creative design work, typing, book-keeping, accountancy, insurance representation. Part-time or full-time service businesses may also be operated *from* the home – for example, window-cleaning, plumbing, odd job work of all kinds, gardening services, decorating, radio and TV repair work.

Full-time service businesses employing staff – and sometimes being subsidiary to the trading business that first sells the equipment for which the after-sales service is provided – normally operate from shops or offices.

It is probable that at some time of their lives almost everybody toys with the concept of independence that is associated with being one's own boss. For those who do not wish to commit themselves too deeply, and for those who want to test out the possibilities, the part-time service business is the most likely to command attention.

A real danger about service businesses, however, is that many people drift into them without an original intention of developing a business. The real beginnings may be in doing a single job for someone, possibly even as a personal favour with no fee suggested or negotiated, but with a subsequent generous payment to cover incurred costs or expenses. Or it may all start with some casual work undertaken to meet a specific expense, without any intention that regular work shall develop as a consequence. From such beginnings fairly regular work may gradually develop, a scale of fees or charges may become established, and a widening circle of clients and an unanticipated reputation may be built up. The point may then come when all these facts compel the eventual decision to go into business on a full-time basis.

Licences, registrations, Income Tax Returns for self-employment earnings, the keeping of proper business records and

Nobody ever became a millionaire on a salary 13

accounting are all responsibilities recognized by the person who, for instance, has always intended leaving his or her wage-earning job when the favourable opportunity occurs. Such a person, perhaps buying a ready-made business of which his accountant has approved, on financial terms of which his bank manager has approved, in a transaction which his solicitor has arranged, has an actual date upon which he commenced his self-employment business – just as an employee has a date upon which his or her employment commenced.

Those drifting into self-employment however may, to begin with, neglect the regulations, only to find themselves facing a worrying situation later instead of celebrating a recognizable point of success. Eventual compliance with all the regulations is inevitable if they are to take their opportunity, but this may mean that previous non-compliance will come to light and the business might be liable to a whole range of penalties.

There is a simple common sense precept to be observed here. If, for example, a neighbour, before going on holiday, asks you to look after the cat – because it is felt that this would be preferable to putting the animal into a cattery – and later persuades you to accept a gift of money no more and no less than would have been paid to the cattery, such a payment would be a personal and private matter between you and your neighbour. If you subsequently put a card in a local shop window which reads, 'Cats and other small domestic pets boarded during holiday periods. Fees reasonable', then you are in business.

There is a simple rule for anyone taking such a first step, however small, hesitant and non-committal, towards self-employment. All details of any earnings – over and above the wage or salary upon which P A Y E has been deducted at source – should be recorded at the time they are made.

The total amount earned, from the date of the first income from this extra source until the following 5 April, should then be disclosed to the Inspector of Taxes on the next Income Tax Return Form, under Schedule D on page 2. This subject is dealt with in detail in Chapter 4. Here it needs only to be emphasized that income should be disclosed to the Inland Revenue even by people who do not consider themselves yet to be in business. Those from whom they earn the income may themselves be required to disclose the details. And, apart from this, if the income develops to a point where the existence of a business venture has to be recognized and disclosed, then the Inspector of Taxes will want to know when it began. And if any one source of income is substantial in the first year the Inspector may wish to investigate the past history of that source.

It is wise, and may well be profitable, to record the establishment of a business as soon as any part-time service work is begun, and the best way of establishing that a business exists, and also of establishing a starting date, is to obtain a Certificate of Registration under the Registration of Business Names Act, 1916. The Department of Trade requires the registration of any business conducted in names other than that of, or those of, the proprietor or proprietors. To take advantage of the fact of registration, which costs a fee of £1, it is therefore necessary to give the business venture a name, which, of course may include the proprietor's name. Thus if John Doe is conducting a business as John Doe, he does not have to register the business. But if he conducts his business as 'Sparkling Windows' or 'Doe's Sparkling Windows' or 'The John Doe Services' he must register. (Wherever the name of John Doe appears in this book to describe a businessman or trader, and wherever the name Richard Roe is used in association with that of John Doe to describe a partnership, the names do not, of course, relate to any living person, persons, partnership or company. The names are chosen because these were the two names used, in English Courts of Law between the time of Edward III and 1852 as convenient fictitious names in Actions of Ejectment which are now only a curiosity of legal history. The American use of the name John Doe was similarly borrowed from English law.)

Here, in discussing the possible drift into self-employment in a service business, it is only necessary to outline the five

Nobody ever became a millionaire on a salary 15

simple, inexpensive steps that anyone may take, leaving all the options open.

1. First obtain Form RBN/1 from the Registrar of Business Names, Pembroke House, 40-56 City Road, London EC1 2DN, and using this register a business name. (The different addresses for Scotland and Wales are given in Chapter 2, which deals in detail with the registration of business names and company registrations.)
2. Order business notepaper in the registered business name.
3. Write a letter to the local Inspector of Taxes, whose address is published in the local telephone directory under the entry 'Inland Revenue'. He should be told that part-time business is intended or has begun, and Form 41G should be requested.
4. Write a letter to the local Social Security Office, listed in the local telephone directory under the entry 'Health and Social Security, Department of' explaining your intentions and asking for leaflets NI27A, NI41, NI42, NI48, and NP18. If you are an employee, you will already be paying Class 1 National Insurance contributions. If you are self-employed even on a part-time basis you also become liable for Class 2 contributions. In certain circumstances you may become liable also for Class 4 contributions. You may apply for exemption in connection with these contributions or you may decide to pay Class 2 voluntarily even if you could be exempt, or may decide to voluntarily pay Class 3 contributions. (Class 2 contributions are collected by the Department of Health and Social Security, Class 4 by the Inland Revenue.)

Full details of this subject are discussed in Chapter 7.

5. Finally write to the VAT office for your area, listed in the telephone directory under 'Customs and Excise Department', again explaining the intention and requesting Form VAT 1. VAT is discussed in detail in Chapter 6, but it needs to be mentioned here in connection with drifting into part-time self-employment.

There is no requirement by HM Customs and Excise that a new business should register for VAT unless the gross turnover is expected to be over £13,500 a year (the current threshold figure), but there may be two very good reasons why VAT registration should be applied for from the very beginning of trading.

In the first place it has to be remembered that Value Added Tax paid by a business to the Customs and Excise is *not* a deduction from the business income. It is a tax collected by the business on its sales on behalf of the Customs and Excise. The business does itself, however, pay VAT on its own purchases whether it is registered or not. It pays it on equipment it buys, even if this is only a filing cabinet. It also pays it on services like the telephone. If the business is registered for VAT it may recover all the VAT it pays itself in connection with the business operation – and yet be collecting much less VAT on behalf of the Customs and Excise. There may therefore be financial advantages in early registration.

The second point hinges on the kind of part-time business being embarked upon. Registering for VAT means, of course, that the charges made for a service, or for what is sold, are increased by the amount of the tax. If the self-employment business is that of part-time gardening, decorating or handyman work and is never going to come within liability for VAT registration, obviously it would be pointless to have to charge a tax as well as a fee to those wanting work done. It would make the service less competitive and when a business is starting the price charged for services is fundamental to becoming established. On the other hand if the service is one being provided to clients themselves registered for VAT, and therefore in a position to reclaim it, and if the clients are likely to be long-term, then it may be advisable to establish VAT registration from the commencement of the service.

In such cases VAT registration is psychologically a bonus as it suggests that the business is serious and successful. More important, in many cases there may be some future date at which, if VAT has not been charged initially, the client charges have to be increased to include it – a situation that has inherent difficulties about it. Where the cost of a service is increased without benefit to the supplier it may rule out any other, normal increase which would have been otherwise acceptable.

Businesses are like buildings, the better for being built upon sound foundations. What may begin as self-employment in a small way is more likely to prosper and develop if given the five-step foundation procedure described – established registration, business notepaper, and files opened on Income Tax, Social Security and V A T.

Success for the part-time beginner often depends on taking the venture seriously, and the surest way of doing that is to ensure that others take it seriously.

SOLE TRADER, PARTNERSHIP or LIMITED LIABILITY?

There is one final categorization of self-employment that must be considered in this general, opening chapter, and which may offer some readers alternatives for consideration. Whatever the type of business (manufacturing, production, trading or service), wherever it is carried out (industrial premises, office, shop or home-base) whether it is part-time or full-time, it may be that of a sole trader, a partnership (usually referred to as a firm) or a limited liability company.

Sole Trader A sole trader works on his or her own as a private individual. You are entirely responsible for your business, although you may employ staff. You may trade under your own name, or under a registered business name. You take all the profits, but you must bear all the losses. If you fail, then your creditors can claim against the value of your home, and all your personal possessions.

This is a situation which best suits some types of service businesses where there are no situations of financial investment risk to run – for example, the freelance writer or artist.

There are many other businesses, however, where it may be desirable to share the responsibilities – but at the cost of sharing the rewards. In this case either a partnership or limited liability company may be formed or acquired.

Partnership A partnership may be formed between two or more people, normally with a maximum of twenty, who carry on a business in common with a view to profit. A Deed of Partnership is not essential, but may be drawn up. In this it is agreed how the profits are to be distributed, how losses will be apportioned if they occur and how the good-will shall be valued in the event of the death, retirement or withdrawal of one of the partners.

Except for certain types of businesses – like those of a general medical practitioner where there are obvious advantages in a group of professional people of equal standing working together on a roster system and pooling specialized aspects of their training, knowledge and experience – partnerships are not common in modern businesses.

The arguments against partnerships are that each partner is legally liable for all the debts of the whole partnership. Thus if one partner enters into a disastrous contract, even if the other partner or partners have opposed the contract, they are legally bound by it. If the consequence is the failure of the business, insolvency and clamorous creditors, as a partner who opposed the contract you may find that not only is your investment in the business lost, but that *your* personal savings, *your* home and *your* private possessions may be forfeit to pay off a list of creditors headed by the Inland Revenue.

Limited Liability Company Because of the personal risk involved in partnerships, limited liability companies have almost entirely replaced them as the arrangement by which several people join together for business purposes. Indeed it is quite common for a businessman who is, in effect, a sole trader to form a company to obtain the benefits of a form of trading in which personal liability is, quite literally, limited in law. By trading as a company, liability for the company's debts is limited to the face value of the shares issued, and private assets are not at risk.

All forms of insurance are secured at cost however, and naturally there are disadvantages to be considered when a decision has to be taken whether to form a limited liability company or not. These are discussed in full in Chapter 2.

THE PERSONAL FACTOR
This introductory chapter has been written to help anyone who proposes to become self-employed decide where to fit himself or herself into the pattern of self-employment. Before going further, however, readers must now ask themselves seriously whether they fit *anywhere* in the pattern. This is a matter of critical self-assessment and has nothing to do with the possession of skills, training, experience, special knowledge, ability, capital or opportunity.

There is, of course, no such thing as a 'typical' small business. Nevertheless as a general rule it has to be recognized that the self-employed have to be self-confident. Neither tiredness, illness, long hours, nor competitive personal interests allow for any let-up for the boss of a business that is succeeding. And there is no standing still. A business is *always* either expanding or losing ground.

If the self-employed do not work, there is no income.

If the work they do is not what is wanted and does not sell, their businesses fail.

If their businesses fail, there is no redundancy 'pay-off'.

The self-employment test This simple, two-question test for any wage or salary earner who hesitates over the decision about self-employment, if answered honestly, will tell you whether you are capable of self-support, regardless of any other requirements.

1. Assume that as an employee there is a wall clock at your place of business. Inevitably you glance at it from time to time towards the end of the day – after all it is there for your information. Do you look to see how much longer you have to work ? Or do you look at it to see how little time you have left?

If you clock-watch for the end of the working day, you are safer with a wage or salary. If you work to beat the clock, then you should be working for yourself.

2. The wall clock at your place of business as an employee is electric and is run off the mains. There has been a power cut and the clock needs a simple resetting adjustment. This is a job done by a team of two staff electricians who have a lot of clocks to reset and will not get around to the one you use until the end of the day. If anybody else – yourself for instance – adjusted the clock, there would be trouble, potentially even a strike.

Does the fact that you may not reset the clock yourself irritate you? Do you think it nonsense, anyway, that a team of two men should be required for this job?

If the answers are 'yes' to both questions, then you show that you have the attitude of mind essential to success in self-employment.

ESSENTIAL ADVISORS
This is the only chapter of the book in which opinion is offered and advice given. It ends with the most important advice of all to any reader who is intending to become self-employed.
Bank Manager Never enter into any financial undertaking without first consulting your bank manager. Even if you have no financial problems to resolve when you are starting your new business venture, you will never know anybody with more money available to help you in the unforeseen emergency than your bank manager. Quite apart from this, the bank probably represents a group of companies which provide a full range of services – including business equipment hire-purchase services, equipment leasing services, insurance services and retirement annuity schemes.
Solicitor Never sign any document, or commit yourself to any agreement either in writing or verbally, without consulting your solicitor. Even if your proposed venture does not involve you immediately in signing legally binding undertakings, it is sensible to put your solicitor in the picture about your intentions. If you do not already have a solicitor, then your bank manager will recommend one who has experience in businesses of the kind you are embarking upon – and this is important. A

solicitor who specializes in divorce is not the man for a shopkeeper.

Accountant Do not commence a new business without discussing the administration and the keeping of records with your accountant. Nobody will *save* you more money than your accountant, so let his fee be the first business expense to claim on your next Tax Return. If you do not already have an accountant, and have no introduction to one, the best course is to consult the *Yellow Pages* Directory and telephone a local firm of accountants – preferably a chartered man with a small practice. Ask his fee for an initial interview and, if this is acceptable, see him and get his general advice about your proposed business. Of all advisers, the accountant is most likely to be in touch with the rough 'catch can' of the market.

Although there are also other specialist professional services to consider, between them, bank manager, solicitor and accountant could give you all the help you will ever need. The accountant will save you more money than his services cost you. The solicitor will save you a great deal of trouble.

This does not mean, however, that you do not have to understand the requirements and the problems of your business. The bank manager, solicitor and accountant will only be as useful to you as you make possible by your communication of relevant information.

Their involvement in most of the content of the rest of the book is, therefore, taken for granted and commented upon only where is it specifically necessary to do so.

2: Forming and registering businesses

BUSINESS NAMES REGISTRATION
Subject to any licences that may be required in connection with particular kinds of businesses, there need be no legal formalities in the United Kingdom about commencing a business either as a sole trader – or, indeed, in a partnership. Unless registered for VAT the sole trader does not even have to keep account books, and he or she does not have to make public any information about the running of the business.

If, however, you conduct your business under a name that in any way differs from your own name, then you must register the name of the business with the Department of Trade's Registry of Business Names.

The addresses are :

England and Wales The Registrar of Business Names
Pembroke House
40-56 City Road
London EC1 2DN (Tel: 01-253 9393)

Scotland The Registrar of Business Names
102 George Street
Edinburgh EH2 3DJ
(Tel: 031-225 5774/5)

Northern Ireland The Department of Commerce
Registry of Business Names
43-47 Chichester Street
Belfast BT1 4RJ (Tel: Belfast 34121/4)

You should furnish particulars of the business within fourteen days of its commencing on the application form RBN/1, obtaining this from your area registry. Failure to register a business entails liability, on conviction, to a fine not exceeding £5 for every day of default, while false statements entail liability on conviction to a term of imprisonment not exceeding three months or a fine not exceeding £20.

A married woman trading under her maiden name must register – so must people who have changed their names after the age of eighteen, or at any time during the previous twenty years.

The registration fee is £1.

Unacceptable names The registrar may refuse to register a business name he considers to be undesirable. Generally speaking this means that 'misleading' names are likely to be rejected.

The words 'Building Society' will not be accepted. Names which suggest a connection with royalty, or use the words 'Royal', 'King', 'Queen', 'Princess' or 'Crown' will not ordinarily be allowed. Names which suggest a connection with a government department, statutory undertaking, local authority, or with any commonwealth or foreign government, or which include the word 'Commonwealth' will not ordinarily be allowed.

The word 'British' is not allowed where, in context with the rest of the business name, it would falsely suggest that the business was pre-eminent in its special business. Nor is it allowed if the business is not British controlled and entirely (or almost entirely) British owned. The same ruling applies to the terms 'National', 'United Kingdom', 'Great Britain', 'Northern Ireland', 'Scotland', 'Europe', 'English', 'Scottish', 'Welsh', or derivatives of these words.

Certain other words are only allowed if investigation by the registrar satisfies him that circumstances justify them. These are the words 'Bank', 'Chamber of Commerce', 'Council', 'Co-operative', 'Corporation', 'Institute', 'Insurance', 'International', 'Investment Trust', 'Register', 'Trust' and 'Unit Trust'. Synonymous and cognate words which by association suggest any of these words are not allowed without justification.

Registration provides a public record, nothing more. It gives no authority to use the name if its use could be prohibited for other than the common sense reasons applied by the registrar. It does not give sole rights in the name. It gives no protection against duplication. It does not necessarily mean that, having registered the name and having traded under it, if at some time later the trader decides to turn his business into a limited liability company, he will be able automatically to register his new company under the established name upon which he has built up the business.

The registrar does not check with the Trade Marks Index whether a business name being registered, or some part of the proposed name, may be protected by a registered trade mark right. To avoid possible later expense and inconvenience it is wise to investigate this possibility before applying for the registration of a business name that could infringe a trade mark right.

The search is made at the Trade Marks Registry, Patents Office, 25 Southampton Buildings, London WC2 1AY (Tel: 01-405 8721).

TRADE MARKS AND PATENTS

The applicant who sees a necessity to protect himself against imitators in his new business – who may be starting business to exploit, manufacture and sell some new product – may register his own trade mark at the Patents Office.

Over 900,000 applications to register trade marks have been made in the UK, since the first one was granted in 1876 to Bass, the brewer. There are currently about 200,000 trade marks in use, and there are about 150 new industrial products every week in the UK, each needing an exclusive identification.

In addition to the words in a name disallowed by the Registrar of Business Names, the Patents Office rules out, in trade mark registrations, geographical names and words which, in describing the nature of a product, could be interpreted as being an officially recognized guarantee of the fulfilment of an advertising claim. A word like 'Soapy', for example, would not be accepted as part of the brand name for a new soap.

A full search for a trade mark name for a new product, which may be marketed internationally, is a long, complex and expensive matter, involving a search of the foreign trade mark registers of 150 countries. Understandably trade mark names are therefore jealously protected.

Trade mark agencies who undertake the necessary arrangements are listed in the *Yellow Pages* directories. For the immediate convenience of readers, one such is Forrester Kettley & Co., Forrester House, Bounds Green Road, London N 11 (Tel: 01-889 6622/6606).

If the new product is the outcome of an invention, that invention may need to be protected by a patent, also registered at the Patents Office. This registration is usually a fairly lengthy procedure, and it involves an investigation of specifications for British patents within the same category for the past fifty years to ensure that the invention has not been claimed, either wholly or in part, by someone else.

Patents are usually taken out through professional patents agents, who have to be registered with the Board of Trade. Such agencies are listed in the *Yellow Pages* directories and often, as in the case of the company to whom reference has been made above in this connection, will appear in both the patents agency and trade marks agency listings.

It should be remembered that even if no trade mark registration is required, when registering a new business name it is wise to ensure that the name does not infringe a trade mark name that has been registered – probably at considerable cost – by someone else.

Consumer credit licences Acceptance by the Registrar of Business Names of an application does not mean that the registered name will necessarily be acceptable for the purposes of the Consumer Credit Act, 1974, if a credit licence is required for the new business, or if one may be required later.

Consumer credit business has recently undergone sweeping change and reform. Very briefly the new Act requires that all businesses involving the giving of credit, or the hiring, renting or leasing of goods now require a licence, although this is currently 'deferred' if transactions involve credit below the sum of £30. The subject of licences is covered fully in Chapter 9. Here, reference is made to the requirement in context with the business names registration.

Many small traders who could not themselves afford to give their customers hire-purchase facilities, introduce their customers to finance companies who provide the service. Such traders, although their involvement in the credit transaction is limited to making the introduction, are now regarded in law as credit brokers, and are required to be licensed as such.

If the proposed business requires, or possibly will require, a consumer credit licence, then it is advisable to consult the Consumer Credit Licensing Branch, the Office of Fair Trading, Government Building, Bromyard Avenue, Acton, London W3 7BB (Tel: 01-749 9151) to make a preliminary enquiry whether the business name it is proposed to register will be acceptable to them.

Once a business name has been registered there are requirements that trade catalogues, circulars, show cards and business stationery carrying the registered name must also carry the names and initials or surnames of all proprietors. The nationality of non-British proprietors must be shown.

In the case of companies – dealt with later in this chapter – the names of all directors must be shown together with other details required by the Companies Act, 1948 and the European Communities Act, 1972.

Any change in the registered particulars should be notified to the registrar within fourteen days. Cessation of business should be notified within three months.

PARTNERSHIPS

A different application form, Form RBN/1A, is required for the registration of a partnership business. Otherwise everything that is applicable to the formation and business names registration of a sole trader business is true of a partnership business.

No formalities are necessary to begin in business as a partnership, subject to any licences that need to be obtained because of the particular nature or circumstances of the business. No books need be kept unless the turnover or anticipated turnover of the business requires registration for VAT, but any business that does not keep clear, detailed books from the very first transaction, is heading for trouble.

Two people may, indeed, go into partnership just by agreeing to do so in a private discussion. Under the Partnership Act of 1890 nothing more is needed. While this fact usefully permits the settlement of disputes that might arise from any single act of 'partnership', the Act is not intended to apply to a serious and continuous business partnership between people who are pooling knowledge, experience, investment and assets into a business venture from which each – or all if there are more than two partners – hopes to profit by their endeavours and industry.

At the very least a written document, signed by each partner, should be exchanged in which the terms of the partnership are set down. Sensibly, a proper Deed of Partnership should be drawn up by a solicitor. This will override the provisions of the simple 1890 Partnership Act, and set out particular agreements about the rights and the responsibilities of each partner. Such a Deed will cover every circumstance in which dispute, resignation or death, by or of one partner, could put a viable business in sudden jeopardy.

As far as the business names registration is concerned, registration of a partnership is required where 'a partnership uses a business name which differs in any way from the true name(s) or the full corporate name(s) of all the partner(s)'.

COMPANY REGISTRATION

The formation and registration of a limited liability company is a much more complex matter than setting up and, as a matter of choice, registering a sole trader or partnership business.

To form a new limited liability company a written application for the name desired must first be submitted to the Companies Registration Office, Companies House, Crown Way, Maindy, Cardiff CF4 3UZ, giving alternatives in order of preference. In Scotland application is made to the Registrar of Business Names, Exchequer Chambers, 102 George Street, Edinburgh EH2 3DJ.

The reasons for which a submitted name either will or may be refused are exactly the same as the reasons why it would or might have been refused for registration as a sole trader or partnership business name – with the additional reason that a company name will be rejected if it is too like that of an existing company or body corporate.

The Companies Registrar, like the Business Names Registrar, does not consult the Trade Marks Index and this prior search should be made by the applicant. At this point there is no fee because approval of a submitted title does not mean that it has been registered and may be used.

The applicant must now prepare for submission the draft Memorandum and Articles of Association. The Memorandum, which forms the company's charter, outlines the full scope of the company's permitted business, allowing for all possible future expansion and diversification. The Articles of Association lay down the administrative arrangements of the company and its management.

These are complex and legally important documents. It is possible to buy 'specimen' drafts from a law stationers – taken from a listing in the *Yellow Pages* directory – which could possibly be adapted by an applicant. If the reader's local directory has no listing, then try: Oyez Stationery Ltd, 191/192 Fleet Street, London EC4 (Tel: 01-405 2847).

The services of a solicitor are never, in any matter, obligatory.

This, however, is one of the circumstances in which professional services may be regarded as virtually essential.
Alternatively, the services of company registration agents, taken from the *Yellow Pages* directory listings, may be engaged. For reader convenience, one such company is Jordans and Sons Ltd, Jordan House, 47 Brunswick Place, London N1 6EE.

When the Memorandum and Articles of Association are submitted, three supporting forms are required with them. These are Form No.1, Form No.41 and Form PUC1. These forms may be obtained, free of charge, either from Companies House, Main Counter, Crown Way, Maindy, Cardiff CF4 3UZ, or from the London Search Room, Special Counter, Ground Floor, 55-71 City Road, London EC1Y 1BB (personal callers only). They may also be obtained from law stationers.

Form PUC1 is a Statement of Capital, required in connection with Inland Revenue capital duty payable on shares issued. Form No.1 is a statement setting out the names and other required information about the directors, secretary and registered office of the company. Form No.41 is a statutory declaration that all the many requirements of the Companies Acts 1948 to 1976 have been complied with. It is usually made and signed by a solicitor, but may be made by a JP or by a director or the secretary of the new company.

Northern Ireland operates its own entirely independent Companies Acts, and enquiries should be addressed to the Registrar of Companies, Department of Commerce, 43-47 Chichester Street, Belfast BT1 4RJ (Tel: Belfast 34121/4).

The registration fee is currently £50, plus Inland Revenue duty of 1% on capital as and when issued – that is £1 on every £100, or part of £100 on the nominal value of the shares issued. To these fees must be added those of the solicitor or company registration agent if the services of either are used. Such fees are likely to be about £100.

A private company's shares cannot be offered to the public, and the company cannot have more than 50 members. It must hold an Annual General Meeting during every calendar year and must make an Annual Return to the registrar, together with a registration fee of £20. It must keep proper accounts with an audited profit and loss account, or income and expenditure account. It must issue a balance sheet at the same time and it must issue a directors' report.

The formation of a new company obviously takes some time, and it is possible to overcome this by buying a 'ready-made' company through a company registration agent. An over-the-counter arrangement of this kind involves formalities that only take a day or two, and the cost in this case will be only about £40. But, of course, such a company also has a ready-made name, and a ready-made Memorandum and Article of Association. It is usually better to let the solicitor or agent establish a company that is tailored in every way to a specific purpose.

A limited liability company needs only to register its business name with the Business Names Registrar if it trades under a business name other than the full corporate name registered with the Registrar of Companies.

For example if our 'John Doe' decides that the advantages of being in business as a limited liability company outweigh the disadvantages, and registers his company as 'John Doe, Ltd' or 'The John Doe Organization Ltd', then, provided he trades under whichever of those names has been registered by the Registrar of Companies, no further business names registration is needed. But if he wants to put the title 'Doe's Sparkling Windows' above any business premises he may have, or on his headed notepaper, thus trading under a different name from that registered by the company, then he must register 'Doe's Sparkling Windows' as a business name.

The registration of the business name of an already registered limited liability company, and all the conditions of registration, and the fee of £1, are the same as for a sole trader or partnership registration, the only difference being that the form to request is Form R B N / 1 B.

It will be clear from the foregoing general outline of the

procedures necessary in the formation of a company, the subsequent requirements and the expenses involved, that any advantages there are in forming a limited liability company may be outweighed by attendant disadvantages.

John Doe as a sole trader, or John Doe and Richard Roe as partners, may have little difficulty in borrowing money from the bank, or in obtaining credit from suppliers. All the sole trader owns, all that either or both of two partners own – home, car, savings tucked away in building societies or in local authority bonds – may be compulsorily sold or realized to pay off debts if the business fails.

But if John Doe Ltd, or Doe and Roe Ltd, fail in business it is not John Doe, or John Doe and Richard Roe who have failed – it is a company which has a legal entity of its own, which may both sue, or be sued. In such a case John, or John and Richard, only lose the face value of the shares they have issued to themselves – perhaps only a nominal £50 each. Nobody can touch their homes, cars, private savings. If, therefore, John Doe's limited liability company needs to borrow money or to make credit arrangements, since the company's liability is limited to its own assets, John Doe may have to guarantee, as an individual, the loan his company needs to borrow.

The pros and cons about the wisdom of forming a company are such that whichever of the three business advisors is the best personal contact at the moment when the decision has to be taken – bank manager, solicitor or accountant – should be asked to give guidance. Often the wise decision will be the one that follows the custom of the particular business.

The term 'limited liability' means that all the members of the company – in practice the shareholders – are protected from being made liable for any greater part of the company's liabilities than the amount they have paid for their shares. It is a protection bought at some cost and its real value is that one member cannot, by misjudgement or default, put at jeopardy all the private possessions of other members, as in the case of a partnership. It also allows a group of supporters

– or shareholders – to provide working capital to a sole trader and to become 'sleeping partners' without putting themselves at any greater risk than the extent of their support.

In general, businesses started by 'teams' of complementary people, each one of whom has some special skill or knowledge to contribute and who becomes responsible for some particular part of the business – thus the producer, the administrator and the salesman make a good team – tend to have a better success record than the lone trader who may be swamped by too great a diversity of responsibilities and tasks. In small industrial operations the limited liability company is generally the ideal basis for such a business partnership.

There is, however, one other aspect of the matter that needs consideration, judgement and a decision that cannot be supplied by the bank manager, the solicitor or the accountant. Business partners need to get along well together, to trust one another and not to have elements of friction in their personal relationships with one another. Personal mistrust and friction are as common a cause of business failures as they are of marriage failures.

3: Capital, finance and funding

CAPITAL NEEDED
The question of how much money is needed to go into business is impossible to answer except in the individual case. No two businesses are exactly the same. No two sets of circumstances are the same. No two people are the same.

John Doe, after proper investigation, buying a small, well situated general shop for £10,000, the price including stock, may have adequate capital if he has £1,000 in reserve, or even if he starts business with a loan of £2,000. Within five minutes of opening on his first day, money is being put into the till.

Richard Roe, on the other hand, as a newspaper staff reporter deciding to become a freelance writer might be very well advised to have up to £12,000 in the bank – even though he is going to work from home and has no equipment to buy because he already has a typewriter. He will be lucky if any money comes in for at least two or three months. He must allow perhaps two, possibly three, years before his income will match his existing standard of living, which may be difficult for him to change.

His sensible approach to the financial side of freelancing might well be to divide his capital into three parts and to live on the first part for the first year, regardless of his earnings. At the end of the first year he then transfers his *net* income for the year – that is after tax – to the remaining two thirds of his original capital, and again divides this by three, taking a resultant one third for his living expenses for the second year.

A system of this kind, adapted to individual needs, ensures that those going into business to provide a professional service can cushion-out the poor performance years while the good years do not result in over-expenditure that may have regrettable effects later.

There are other businesses, of course, where the critical factor upon which success depends is a personal ability to deal with financial problems in an unorthodox way. The late Lord Thomson, when he had his first Canadian businesses in North Bay and Timmins, paid his North Bay employees with cheques on a bank account opened in Timmins to give himself three days clearance time to raise and deposit funds to meet his payroll. In Timmins, if funds were adequate, the staff was paid in cash. If funds were neither high nor low the staff was paid half in cash and half by cheque. If there was no money in the bank, salaries were paid by cheques which the employees cashed with Brunette the taxi driver, Sutherland the druggist, or the Chinese restaurant owner, all of whom had a tacit agreement to hold the cheques back until there was money to cover them. Roy Thomson was not the only man to walk such a financial tight-rope to the attainment of millions, but such a course is not recommended. Even by exceptional men it is trodden only with risk.

What *is* true is that it is essential, before going into business, to work out very carefully exactly what capital will be needed to begin the business and what reserve funding must be available thereafter.

If an established business is being bought, much of what the purchase money is largely paying for – the 'goodwill' – is the reasonable assumption that the kind of turnover and kind of income that the business has had up to the day of its transfer will continue. A legal judgement on goodwill once was that it was 'nothing more than the likelihood that customers will resort to the old place'.

Even so there may be the cost of premises, mortgages or rent. There may be new equipment costs. There will be the cost of rates, heating, lighting, insurance, stock replenishments, stationery, licences, professional fees, and possibly wages, advertising and transport. Finally, there will be personal and domestic needs. All these costs have to be considered in terms of initial capital outlay and in terms of continuing expenses.

It is much cheaper, in terms of capital investment, to start any new business from scratch. Many businesses have to be started in this way, but these are, however, the businesses that are very vulnerable to failure because of a lack of capital reserves. How long it will take for a new business to become viable is a matter for individual judgement. What can be said is that it almost always takes much longer than the most cautious of forecasts. More new sole-trader businesses fail because of inadequate reserve funds than for any other reason. There are circumstances and situations where, if an opportunity is not to be missed, it may be necessary to borrow money to launch the business. Generally speaking, this is not a sound way to begin. It means that from the start, during the 'difficult' period, there is both capital and interest to be repaid.

BANKING SERVICES

Even if no loan is needed initially, and there are reserve funds to keep things going until the business establishes itself, it is sensible to realize from the beginning that these reserves *may* prove to be inadequate.

It is not the best time to start looking round for financial help when a business is in trouble, and a rescuing loan is needed. This is why, before the first steps are taken to go into business, it is sensible to discuss the venture with the bank manager.

A bank's services to the small businessman are not as widely understood as they should be. The basic service is, of course, a business account. Costs for small business accounts are inevitably assessed according to the work involved in running the account. Because the term 'small business' covers a wide range of businesses it is not possible here to suggest typical charges; but the bank manager, when such an account is being opened, will be able to give some idea of a budget figure.

The business account affords the following facilities:

1. Free cheque forms and credit forms – that is, all the forms needed for 'paper' transfers of money in and out of the account.
2. Regular statements of the account.
3. Bankers Order and Direct Debit facilities.
4. Branch offices throughout the country with night safe deposit services at the majority of them (for example, National Westminster has over 3,300 branch offices with night safes at about 85% of them).
5. Numerous ancillary advisory services, for the most part free.
6. Contact with financial services and sources of finance for current business and future expansion, including fixed credit facilities like Access and Barclay's Visa Barclaycard.

Banks – and this is also true, in the same connection, of insurance companies, finance houses and mortgage brokers – are in business themselves, and their business is money. Someone else going into business is a potential 'customer' to them. Whether the customer is going to succeed or fail in his or her own business, the bank expects to make a profit and will protect itself against incurring any loss.

A bank will always welcome sound business, and will be helpful on principle. It does not want profitable business to go elsewhere. Do not, therefore, be inhibited in your dealings with your bank manager. Do, however, understand his position. Services the bank and its subsidiaries can give at ordinary fees present no problem. If you require to borrow money, however, you are asking the bank manager to share your risk of failure, but not your reward of success.

The money the bank has available to lend belongs to depositors. If the bank lends you money and your business fails, and you cannot repay the loan, the bank still has to repay that money to its depositors eventually, and meanwhile has to continue paying interest upon it as if it were still there. On the other hand if your business succeeds, and eventually you repay the loan, the bank itself has to pay part of the interest it charged you to its depositors and has to cover its administrative costs. Its own profit is quite small. A bank, therefore, will normally require first a sufficient knowledge of you and your business before it will even consider making a loan.

Merchant banks are not generally likely sources of finance for new businesses, unless loans of at least £25,000 are involved. It is the big joint-stock clearing banks, like National Westminster or Midland who are the major source of finance for small businesses.

The bank manager who gives help is, in a sense, a business partner and should be treated as such. It is sensible, before meeting him to discuss the matter, to outline and describe your proposed business and 'sell' the idea of it to him as sound, just as you would if you were inviting a partner to join you.

Do this by letter first, asking for an interview. A letter gives time for consideration, for investigation into the way in which you have conducted your account in the past, and possibly for enquiries about the kind of business you propose and the locality in which you may intend to operate. In the letter you have to make it quite clear what help you want – whether you need it now, or whether you merely want to prepare the ground for possible later tide-over help.

The bank manager will give you sound financial advice and will do his best to be helpful. Always listen to him.

If he is to make a loan, the bank manager will expect security in the form of assets. For the reasons already explained he is not in a position to risk any share of a possible failure of your venture. These securities may be on any equipment for the new business, they may be on personal insurance and endowment policies, they may be on your home and other private property assets. If you have the assets, you can usually count on getting the loan.

In the case of a limited company, where the loan would be to the company, the borrower, as a director, would be required to guarantee the loan to the company by pledging his own personal assets. Where loans are secured by assets possessed by the company, and not the proprietor, there is a device known as a 'floating loan', which allows the 'security' to be dependent on the assets of the company at any one time as opposed to listed assets existing at the time of the loan.

OVERDRAFTS

The most common form of a bank loan to a small business is a simple overdraft.

An overdraft has an agreed ceiling amount and is normally arranged *provisionally* for a short term, generally a year. The business can draw up to the limit, and pays interest not on the whole amount of overdraft granted, but on the actual amount being used – and then only on a day to day basis for the period that the account is 'into the overdraft'. Thus, if there were an agreement that you, the client, could borrow up to £3,000 on your business account, but during the course of a year you only once went 'into the red' and then for only £200, and on this occasion for only two days, then you would only pay loan interest on the £200 for two days – and the interest would be between $2\frac{1}{2}\%$ and 3% above the bank's base rate at that time.

There could be no better or cheaper financial support arrangement, but the snags are that base rates fluctuate constantly, and overdraft facilities are always liable to be suddenly withdrawn. Here is where a bank manager's personal assessment of you as a businessman and your business becomes of importance. If the business has been 'living on its overdraft', that is, has constantly been taking the full loan and regarding it as part of the business capital, the bank manager will be less sympathetic than to a business which has used the loan facilities from time to time but has also at times been significantly in credit.

TERM LOANS

Banks may also offer 'term loans'. One such scheme, National Westminster's Business Development Loan Scheme, provides loans from between £2,000 and £100,000 for fixed terms of up to seven years. The bank will need good evidence of the viability of the business to grant such a loan. The interest rates, which are subject to change, will be higher than on an overdraft, and interest will be paid on the whole sum whether it is being used or not. Business development loans normally call for monthly repayments over five years, or exceptionally over seven years.

In cases where he is not able to help, the bank manager is the best possible advisor about other sources of finance that may provide the solution.

TRADE CREDIT

For certain types of businesses – specifically trading businesses – the conventions of trade credit may suffice to overcome a situation of what is, really, inadequate capital. Although business dealings between individual people are normally on a hard-cash basis, between businesses it is customary for there to be a settlement period, often a period of one month.

This in effect may mean that traders can buy goods from their suppliers without having the money to pay for them, but knowing that in the normal way of business they will have sold at least enough of the goods to meet their debts by the time their payment has to be made.

There are three points to be borne in mind here.

1. If the business being commenced is one which itself customarily gives trade credit for the goods or services it supplies, then the trade credit obtained from, say, a raw materials supplier has to be balanced against the credit that has to be given to the client-trader who is being supplied. The difference between being a net recipient of trade credit and being a net supplier can be the difference between the success or failure of the business.

2. The newcomer into any manufacturing or producing business in which, to be competitive, he or she must offer the customary terms of credit – often suggested by that industry's trade association – should be aware of the fact that his or her

clients will usually tend to pay big, well-established suppliers promptly and smaller newcomers less promptly. There is no business reason behind this fact. It is simply the way things are.
3. It must always be remembered that no credit is obtained without cost. A common trade custom is for the supplier to offer the trader one month's credit, with a 2% discount for immediate settlement – that is within one week. A 2% discount sacrifice may not seem, on the face of it, a dear way of getting an extra three weeks' grace before settling the account with the proceeds from goods that may have by then been sold to the public. But £2 to cover a loan of £100 for three weeks really means that the trader is paying £34.7% per annum on the gap-bridging financing of his or her business. And that is not good business!

It is a good rule to remember that, since you are in business to make money, try not to waste it. In short, never miss a discount.

FUND BORROWING

One problem that may lie ahead for the new business is that success may involve unexpected expansion in anticipation of increased business. The business may have been soundly financed when it was commenced but now it has to travel on the tide of its success and capital for further expansion has not had time to build up yet. Mushroom growth of a new business can be dangerous.

The accountant, assuming one has been engaged from the outset, is likely to have advised working to a six months budget, showing, on a monthly basis:

1. Anticipated receipts.
2. Anticipated outgoings, distinguishing between known and probable liabilities.

Such a budget will predict a 'cash flow' position and show where the troughs are likely to occur.

The accountant will also have advised certain types of

funding – which are commonsense necessities for even the small-time part-timer who has put off engaging professional advice because the volume of business does not yet seem to justify it.

Retained profits The first of these funds is known as retained profits. This fund is simply that part of the net profits put aside, not taken by the businessman for his own use, not issued to any shareholders in a company, but earmarked as true business capital. Retained profits are available for expansion, but may be inadequate if the business is growing rapidly.

Depreciation charges The second fund is described on annual accounts as depreciation charges. Depreciation charges are agreed with the Inland Revenue and represent the depreciation of the value of business assets – ranging from the home typist's typewriter to the manufacturer's industrial machinery or the travelling representative's van or business car. In theory, by the time such fixed assets are worn out, or have become technologically inadequate and are due to be replaced, the deductions funded over a period of years will provide for their replacement. When there are not yet any retained profits or where they are inadequate, the business may 'borrow from itself' in an emergency, by using the accumulated depreciation charges sinking fund. But such borrowing has to be replaced, and although the 'loan' may seem to be advantageous in that it carries no interest, it has to be regarded as short-term.

Rolling liabilities The third and final fund is one which *must* be put aside from all gross turnover income as it comes in, by even the smallest home-based, part-time supplier of services where there are no retained profits, and no equipment or assets requiring a depreciation fund.

These are funds set aside to meet known financial commitments due in the near future. The most common part of such funding is that put aside to pay to the Inland Revenue for Income Tax, the Customs and Excise for VAT (where there is VAT registration), Corporation Tax in the case of limited companies as opposed to sole traders and partners who have not formed companies, and Capital Gains Tax if any is involved.

All these are commitments on business that has happened as opposed to anticipated expenditure in connection with future business. If such funds are used, perhaps to avoid the cost in interest of an outside loan, they must be for short-term necessities only.

PRIVATE INVESTOR LOANS

Finance can, in certain circumstances, be borrowed from private investors – people who are known to the borrower, or who may be introduced to him or her by a solicitor or accountant. This is not a recognized 'business' source of finance. Money of this kind is only fortuitously available. It is usually 'dear' money, too.

Such sources of money should be regarded as a possible necessity in a gap-bridging emergency. They should not be used for launching a new business.

FACTORING

Another form of trade credit to which reference must be made is known as factoring. Factoring credit firms are listed in the *Yellow Pages*. They may be recommended by the bank. They may be a subsidiary of the bank, to whom application should therefore be made first.

A factoring service is a specialist organization that takes over the sales accountancy operation of a business, eliminating the costs, the staff and the administrative problems of maintaining a sales ledger. It issues the invoices, and it is responsible for collecting payments from the firm's clients for the goods or services the firm has supplied. Provided the factoring company approves of the clients whom the firm is dealing with, it gives the firm a complete guarantee against bad debts.

The factor may make regular period payments based upon the firm's sales record, regardless of its own collection of debts from the firm's clients. In some cases, if the volume of business justifies it, the factor may advance up to 80% of the value of future sales at the time the business takes delivery of new stock, a facility that releases funds otherwise tied up in trade credit. And, as the business grows so, just one step in advance of the growth, the availability of finance from the factor company grows.

Sometimes the firm's clients may not welcome the existence of a specialist 'debt collecting' organization, in which case the factor company may remain discreetly in the background, appointing the client as its 'agent' to collect the debts, but doing all the work and management and organization itself.

The factoring service is an ideal arrangement for certain businesses where the business proprietors may wish to restrict their interest to the job and work they know and not be bothered by problems of financial administration. But of course they must pay for the 'partnership' provided.

Generally, factoring firms provide the service for businesses with a turnover of about £200,000 a year. Where they undertake to provide the service for firms having a smaller turnover, then they expect good evidence that the business is a sound one with good growth prospects.

The service is expensive and costs between 1% and $2\frac{1}{2}$% of sales, which means that the administration and invoicing and collection of income may cost between £2,000 and £5,600 a year in a £200,000 turnover, while financial facilities which provide cash before it has been collected are at interest rates as high as 4% over the current base rate.

Factoring services are available only for business conducted with manufacturers, wholesalers and retailers – not for business with the consumer market or final purchaser.

Some of the smaller factoring businesses will extend their facilities in a special way to small firms, providing an invoice discounting service. This means that they will advance up to 75% of the amount for which the firm is sending out invoices, provided the firm's clients are approved, allowing a debt collecting lag of an agreed term, possibly two months. This is, of course, simply a short-term financial loan of 75% of what is owed to the business by its clients.

BUSINESS HIRE-PURCHASE

Another form of financial credit that has obvious importance, whether going into business requires the purchase of a typewriter or of a fleet of coaches, is hire-purchase.

Business hire-purchase has some aspects in which it differs from ordinary domestic hire-purchase conducted through a shop, possibly with a finance house. The same general principles apply of course. The buyer of the equipment enters into an agreement with the finance house to hire the equipment for an agreed period with the option, then, to purchase for a purely nominal sum. The equipment, at any moment of the agreement, has a greater re-sale value than the amount the buyer still owes on it. It always has a longer 'life expectancy' at any time than the remaining terms of the hiring agreement.

Where business equipment is involved, the business is able to obtain the same tax allowances as it would have had if the equipment had been bought for cash. The finance charges are also eligible for tax relief.

BLOCK DISCOUNTING

Finance companies also offer small businesses a service by which the business can offer rental schemes or credit payment schemes to customers under their own business name although in fact the finance company 'buys' the agreements for cash from the business at an agreed interest rate of about $1\frac{1}{2}\%$ per month. Such arrangements are known as block discounting facilities.

In a somewhat similar way a finance house may meet the cost of special sales promotions schemes, in return for which any resulting hire-purchase business is given to them by the trader.

EQUIPMENT LEASING

Hire-purchase is designed to produce ultimate ownership of the equipment. Equipment leasing is an alternative which encourages maximum use of the equipment – on the argument that profits are earned from the use of equipment and not from the ownership of it.

The distinction between the terms 'hire' and 'leasing' belong to modern business terminology. In fact the two words are not synonymous but complementary. One person hires and the other leases.

In business equipment leasing, the hirer is never going to own the equipment which he agrees to rent from the finance company for a fixed period for a fixed rate of rental. Leasing, where it is possible, has the advantage to the leasing business that, because the finance company can claim all capital allowances and any grants there may be, the effect is to lower the rent to the renting business. At the same time the rentals in a leasing contract are chargeable against profit and so diminish income tax payable to the renter.

Leasing can apply to any capital equipment ranging from the £500 office machine to a fleet of aircraft. Very typical is the leasing of 'complete office equipment and furnishing'.

Such leases usually consist of two periods. The first is a primary period, the term of which is linked to an anticipated useful life of the equipment during which it is not expected to become obsolete. The lessees have the benefits of using the equipment in a maximum way without a large capital outlay, their rentals being fixed in advance for the whole term. When this primary period comes to an end a secondary period may be negotiated to allow for further use of the equipment if it still has a useful working life. During this period the rentals may be nominal.

Costs are variable and are decided on the credit rating of the applicant. Small, new businesses usually pay higher leasing rates – if they can secure them at all – than large, soundly established businesses.

MORTGAGES

Capital can, of course, be raised by property mortgages, thus turning a property asset into working capital. Where business premises are involved, arrangements of this kind are usually made to procure an injection of extra capital to allow an existing business to expand, and such mortgages are usually for at least £20,000. A business may also sell its property, to get its full current market value, on lease-back terms under which the business remains in occupation as a tenant.

The small business owner either beginning business, or needing to 'survive' while the business establishes itself, can always, of course, take out a mortgage or a second mortgage on his or her home. If such a move has to be considered, this is a matter for discussion first with the bank manager, who may have more advantageous recommendations to make.

INNOVATION CAPITAL AND VENTURE CAPITAL

The inventor who has an entirely new product which he or she wants to produce and put on the market may seek what is known as innovation capital. Specialist finance companies will provide money both to develop prototypes and/or to make production models of new products.

This sort of finance is usually available for the development and production of relatively small products, and loans are generally around the £30,000 level. In arrangements of this kind the loan is made at current rates of interest, and the interest is charged on the amount of the outstanding loan at any time. Repayment of the loan and the accrued interest begins when the product is marketed and a cash flow starts.

The inventor is also required to form a limited company if this has not already been done, and part of the arrangement is that the finance company will have a minority shareholding in this.

The idea of the lender becoming involved in the borrower's business as a shareholder also applies in cases of what is known as venture or development capital. In these cases the capital is provided either to new firms with good prospects, or to existing businesses having high profits but needing capital to exploit their potential.

Loans – either by individuals, or merchant banks, or international finance organizations – are usually for not less than £40,000. The venture-capital finance company will not only require a share issue in the company, but may require to appoint a non-executive director to the board of the company.

Usually this kind of investment loan is made on the assumption that the private company will grow in a few years to a size at which it will 'go public' and have its shares quoted by the Stock Exchange and issued to the general investing public. This is what the venture or development capital financiers are looking for. When they make their loan, they are already anticipating selling their holding of shares at high profit when the business has been built up and allows a free current-market-value sale of shares by having gone public. An overall return of 30% per annum compound interest on the investment loan is likely to be required. The rewards may be very high, but this form of financing is not for the small business at its launch, or for the person who hopes simply to earn a good standard of living from his or her venture.

Indeed the biggest venture/development company is the Industrial and Commercial Finance Corporation Ltd (ICFC), which was set up in 1945 by the English clearing banks, the Scottish clearing banks and the Bank of England. Its capital investment in companies is probably bigger than all the other institutional venture/development investing companies put together, and it probably has a major finger-in-the-pie in over two thousand businesses. As a general rule its partnership exercises a much looser rein than other such lenders require upon their investment partners. Also as a general rule the ICFC lends at lower rates, and does not sell out without agreement by the major shareholders.

Technical Development Capital Ltd (TDC) is a subsidiary of ICFC and exists to invest capital in new companies wanting to launch the production of new inventions or new processes. Both these two bank-controlled companies will invest smaller sums than are usual in this kind of financing – as low as £5,000 against the usual £30,000 to £50,000 minimum.

Such specialized types of business financing form a very

complex and constantly changing pattern. The reader of this book must be made aware of them, but the bank manager is the best guide through the maze to any particular kind of financial aid needed at a given time.

OTHER SPECIAL BANKING SERVICES

There are companies which specialize in providing finance simply for the vehicles a business may need. Such organizations act as a kind of specialist equipment leasing organization, leasing just one particular piece of equipment, whereas equipment leasing businesses normally buy for leasing whatever the client business needs.

Vehicle leasing organizations look after all the transport problems of the business, leasing the required vehicles, looking after costs of maintenance, road fund licences and insurance. Other companies exist which provide short-term loans for the motor trade to provide capital needed for 'stocking'.

Banks may also offer computerized payroll services which handle all the input documents, pay slips (pre-sealed in security envelopes), payroll, financial reports on National Insurance, and costing reports. This is a service normally used by firms with fifty or more employees being paid weekly or monthly, but firms with smaller staffs are sometimes accepted.

Chapters 7 and 8 deal with insurance and pensions, but it is in context with a general survey of the financial services offered by banks to mention that the bank may have a subsidiary company dealing with insurance matters of all kinds. In these matters the bank acts as the insurance brokerage company, although it may operate retirement annuity schemes in conjunction with one of the big insurance companies.

No business of any size – from the home-based, part-time venture to the largest and most ambitious projects – can operate without using clearance bank facilities. Since the most fundamental financial requirement is a banking account, it makes sense to use all or any of the other bank services that are available and may be required – beginning with an interview with the bank manager. In business financial matters, if the bank manager cannot help he always knows who can or may do – if the business proposition seems to him to be a sound one.

4: Income Tax

The United Kingdom is subject to one of the world's harshest and most severe taxation systems. For the great majority of people, however, this is a situation to be suffered but not one which imposes any need on their part for an understanding of our cumbersome and complex fiscal regulations with all their ambiguities, hurdles, pitfalls and loopholes.

The great majority, being in gainful employment, have their earnings taxed at source through PAYE, under Schedule E. Any unearned income they have usually comes from savings invested with building societies or in local authority bonds. The dividends they receive from such sources have already had the tax deducted. As for VAT, it is simply an unseen part of the cost of almost all purchases and services, and the question of recovering any part of the tax does not arise for them.

But the moment the employees go into business on their own account, on whatever scale and whether part-time or full-time, it is a whole new ball game, their self-employment earnings being taxed under Schedule D.

The differences are these:

First: When John Doe was an employee his employer had to deal on his behalf with the Inland Revenue, find out how much tax John would have to pay, on average, each week or month on his wage or salary, until the end of the fiscal year. The employer then had to make the correct deduction from the weekly wage packet or monthly salary cheque and be responsible for paying the tax to the Inland Revenue. All John ever had to do was, once a year, fill in a form giving details of any insurances or mortgages he held, or other straightforward circumstances that might affect his tax.

The employer also dealt with the Department of Health and Social Security for him, and the employer invariably engaged expert accountants to deal with all these complex responsibilities.

The moment John Doe earns some money by gainful self-employment, however, all these responsibilities become his.

Second: John's employer had a relatively simple task in paying John's Income Tax for him. It could be assumed that John's wage or salary would remain the same for the rest of the year and that any allowances would remain constant, since the only allowances John could claim were for ongoing commitments or responsibilities – mortgages, insurances, dependent relatives. This meant that a fixed percentage deduction could be applied to all wage or salary payments made to John, the balance being paid to the Inland Revenue.

But when John earns his first money from any self-employment work, he does not know how much he is going to earn between then and the end of the fiscal year. He cannot know what allowances he may qualify for or what expenses he may incur. He is going to have to pay tax on what he has earned, but nobody knows how much yet. Nobody wants any part of the money in his pocket either at the end of the week or the end of the month. Indeed once his business is established, if John Doe earns his first money on 6 April it may be one year and ten months before he actually pays half the tax due on his first self-employment earnings and two years and four months before he pays the other half.

This is a self-employment situation that lies behind much human anxiety and despair, especially in the world of entertainment where the peaks and troughs of income are unpredictable, and may involve great extremes, and where expenses are not only high but so individual that whether they are going to be allowable for tax purposes or not may be very debatable.

Such people find it difficult to put aside funds from current income to pay tax at some very distant future date – especially when they have no idea how much to put aside, anyway. And even if they do 'fund' money wisely for the purpose, they may be tempted to raid that fund when they next hit an income trough.

Third: John, as an employee, was not concerned with all the complex structure of business allowances and expenses. The moment he is earning on his own account, however, whether he buys a spade to dig a client's garden, or an airliner to run charter flights, whether he puts a card advertising his services in a local shop window, or takes time on commercial T V for an advertising campaign – every time he spends money with the intention of making money, then he is in the area of deductions and allowances (which are not the same thing !). And since most of such spending will involve paying V A T he has the further consideration of regaining the separate tax paid in this way.

One may make this opening conclusion. John Doe may have been a valued employee whose trained capabilities well equipped him to go into business on his own account and to be highly successful in producing a product or giving a service for which he will easily and quickly find a market or clientele.

But the marginal difference between viability and failure, between being relaxed and glad to be independent or of being tense and full of perpetual anxieties, may well depend upon the struggle to understand, cope with and turn to best advantage, the whole matter of taxation.

And it should be said here that the average Income Tax Inspector has a sympathetic understanding of the problems of the John Does of self-employment.

FINDING AND DEALING WITH AN ACCOUNTANT

It is clearly important that those in business on their own account should obtain the maximum advantages of available tax-free benefits and should gain every permitted allowance and expenditure deduction.

The Board of Inland Revenue publish a leaflet (IR 28 – Starting a Business) in which the following comment is made:

> 'Whether to engage an accountant is something you are free to decide for yourself. It is not essential, but it is an advantage to have a qualified professional accountant to advise you on day-to-day book-keeping, payment of National Insurance contributions, Value Added Tax, the operation of PAYE and financial matters generally, as well as to audit your books, draw up your accounts, and agree with the Inspector of Taxes the amount of your taxable profit.'

Since it is part of the business of the accountant to reduce the amount of tax his clients might well pay if they did not have professional advice, such a recommendation by the Inland Revenue itself argues the case for employing an accountant with greater force than if the argument came from any other source.

That the self-employed should follow this recommendation is not without value to the Inland Revenue, who 'have their work cut out' even when returns and accounts are handled professionally. Each year, and sometimes twice yearly, there are Finance Acts which make considerable changes in taxation law. It is the accountant's professional job to keep up to date with these changes and also to have regard to judicial decisions in the cases which are summarized in professional journals.

This does not mean that this chapter could be reduced to the advice: 'Get an accountant and leave it to him!'

First get your accountant. Then know how to deal with him. Finally, and above all, understand exactly what he is doing for you, can do for you, and what the result will be. You are the one who has to fund for future tax payments, and you need to have a rough idea at the time you earn the money how much of it is really yours. You are the one running the business, and only you know what equipment you need. You have to know and understand about capital allowances yourself, even if you leave the figure work and the arguing to the accountant.

An accountant may be selected from the *Yellow Pages* directory. He may be recommended by the bank manager, or by the solicitor – and all recommendations have value. Or he may be recommended by someone in the same kind of business who has been using his services for some time. This is probably the best way to find a suitable accountant.

Accountants can, of course, deal with the affairs of any kind of business. On the other hand the business intricacies of a racing stables, for example, and of a pop group by contrast, are clearly very different. An accountant who has racing stables, trainers and owners among his clients is clearly likely to be of more value to someone going into business in any aspect of horse racing than to someone in the recording business where allowances and expenses are linked to the peculiarities of life 'on the road' and in which the term 'gig' has nothing to do with a horse-drawn vehicle. Getting the right kind of accountant may be important, especially where the business is in any way specialist or is not offering a commonplace service.

Any good accountant, however, will regard it as an essential part of his service to save his clients, in one way or another, more than the fee he charges them. Indeed, in the case of big businesses, what is professionally known as 'tax minimization' – or more commonly 'tax avoidance' – often occupies more time on the part of accountants and tax consultants than would be spent by the business in creating a sum of profit similar to the saving. It may be a sad commentary on the structure of our contemporary society that this is so, but we have to deal with facts as they are.

It has been said that while an accountant must be chosen with the same sense of judgement as a man should choose a mistress, or a woman a lover, thereafter the accountant should be treated as a priest in the confessional box.

In law it is you, the trader, who is responsible for the accuracy of the accounts your accountant prepares and submits to the Inland Revenue, and it is your, the trader's responsibility for a correct declaration of the amount of your profits. But an accountant's reputation with the Inland Revenue is a valuable asset both to himself and to all of his clients. Clients who deliberately conceal facts about their business, their expenses and their profits from their accountant, hoping that by using an accountant's services they may have the shelter of a reputation for reliability to get away with tax evasion, are not only dishonest (which is a matter for their own conscience), but they are endangering the professional reputation of the accountant and, in consequence, the accountant's value to all his other clients.

It cannot be urged too strongly here that if the services of an accountant are engaged, then every penny of income – even the non-traceable, crumpled bank notes – must be revealed to the accountant. There is nothing naive about giving this advice. It is simple common sense, even for the 'tax dodger'!

There have been, and will continue to be, cases where a businessman sells his home to his company, then is allowed to rent it back at a minimal charge for ten years; after which – when its value has been dramatically inflated – he is entitled to buy it back at the original figure for which he sold it. Thus he has lived virtually rent-free for ten years, and the inflationary increase on the value of the property during that time becomes a tax-free profit when he takes up his option to repurchase his house.

However, the rent paid will be brought into the limited company's tax computation for Corporation Tax, and the Inland Revenue will assess the difference between the rent paid and the annual value of the premises. This difference will be classed as director's benefit and the director will be assessed under the Finance Acts of 1976 and 1977. Moreover, if the house is disposed of after it has been repurchased by the director there will probably be loss of exemption of Capital Gains Tax. The gross annual value of the house for rating purposes will be increased and additional rates will be payable.

It is rather like a game of chess. The tax consultants find a loophole and begin to operate it and the Treasury makes a counter-move that cancels out the 'dodge'.

Publicity has been given to other instances of well-dressed businessmen whose £250 suits belong not to themselves but to their companies. The company sells the 'second-hand suit' back to the tailor for £20 at the end of the year, and the tailor then sells it to the man who has been wearing it for a year for £25. The scheme is currently under examination by the Inland Revenue, and it could well be dealt with under a future Finance Act with retrospective legislation. It is also vulnerable to VAT problems.

These schemes are only two of many devised by tax consultants for the victims of success who had reached a point where they were handing over to the Inland Revenue 83% of their upper-level earned income, until the rate was reduced in the June 1979 budget to 60% (bringing it roughly into line with the European average).

It is no use moralizing over the impropriety of such legal 'dodges'. It should merely be observed that the rules of this strange game demand that not one penny of income should be undeclared, nor one penny of due tax evaded.

These examples are given as background to show that most of the means by which the self-employed may reduce the burden of tax are actually devised for them not by shrewd accountants but by statutory provisions. These provisions are the recognized allowances and expenses that this chapter is concerned with, for it has to be said that 'avoidance' devices, for which the taxpayer may pay heavy professional fees, usually end up with the taxpayer in a worse state than at the beginning.

STEP BY STEP GUIDE TO INCOME TAX RESPONSIBILITIES

As soon as you start work on your own account you should tell your local Inspector of Taxes. This may not be the same Inspector or the same office that dealt with your PAYE if you have been, or are also continuing to be, in employment. You should communicate with the Inspector of Taxes for your home address area, whose address appears in the local telephone directory under the heading 'Inland Revenue'.

Tell him what you are proposing to do and ask for pamphlet IR 28. He will send you this, anyway, because it contains Form 41 G which you have to fill in and send back to him. This form, actually your 'passport' into self-employment, is reproduced on page 58 to show the initial information that will be required from you.

Next, you should write to the local office of the Department of Health and Social Security who need to know about your new status as a self-employed person for National Insurance contributions purposes. This should be done even if you are continuing to work as an employee and only doing extra, spare-time or part-time work for yourself. Chapter 7 deals with the self-employed persons involvement with the Department of Health and Social Security. It is, however, in context in a chapter dealing exclusively with Income Tax, to refer to one aspect of National Insurance contributions.

In addition to the flat-rate Class 2 contributions which are normally payable by all self-employed or part-time self-employed who are below retirement age, you may also become liable for payment of Class 4 contributions. Unlike the other three classes of National Insurance contributions, the Class 4 contributions are both assessed by the Inland Revenue and collected by them at the same time as they collect tax payable on self-employment earnings. The Class 4 contribution rate is currently 5% of profits or gains between £2,250 and £7,000, with a maximum of £237.50. The contribution is not payable, however, by men over the age of sixty-five, or women over the age of sixty.

There are certain circumstances, explained in Chapter 7, in which you may be allowed deferment from Class 4 contributions. These may arise if you expect to remain both employed and self-employed, anticipate a substantial income as an employee, and could, therefore, 'overpay' on Class 2 and Class 4 contributions. In this case you ask for Form CF 359

ENQUIRIES	REPLIES
1. In what name is the business carried on, if not in your own name?	1.
2. (a) What is the business address if different from your private address? (b) What is your private address?	2. (a) (b)
3. What is the nature of the business?	3.
4. When did you start in this business?	4.
5. If you took over an existing business, from whom did you acquire it?	5.
6. Have you any partners? If so, please give their names and private addresses.	6.
7. To what date do you propose to make up your business accounts? If they are to be prepared by an accountant, please give his name and address.	7.
8. If you are not already operating PAYE as an employer, have you any employees earning: (a) more than £15.50 a week? (b) at least £15 but not more than £15.50 a week? (c) more than £1 a week who have other employment?	8. (a) (b) (c)
9. If in addition to running your business you are in paid employment, or are continuing an existing business, please give particulars.	9.
10. (a) If you have left employment, please state the name and address of your employer and the date you left. If you still have the leaving certificate form P45 handed to you by your last employer, please attach it. (b) If you have discontinued another business please state the nature and address of that business and the date it ceased.	10. (a) (b)
11. If you have previously made a tax return, please state: (a) the name of the Tax Office to which you made it. (b) the reference number in that Office. *If you are a married woman the answers to question 11 should relate to your husband. If you cannot give these particulars, state the name and address of your husband's employer or his business address.*	11. (a) (b)

Full name .... Date ....
(In BLOCK letters)
(*If you are a woman state whether single, married, etc., and if married, give your husband's Christian or other forenames* ....)

from either your local Inspector of Taxes, or the Department of Health and Social Security and make an application on this form for deferment. If deferment is granted then calculation and collection of the Class 4 contributions is transferred from the Inland Revenue to the Department of Health and Social Security.

Deferment allows postponement of payment until the end of the year so that the liability may be worked out on the basis of the actual income earned.

THE TRADING YEAR

The date to which a self-employed person makes up his or her accounts is a matter of personal choice. You may date your accountancy year from the date you went into business on your own account, and regard your accountancy year as always ending on the anniversary of that date.

You may, whenever you start trading, make your accounts up to the end of each calendar year, 31 December. If your business is one which has a seasonal slack period, you may choose to do your accounts up to an annual date during such a period. Or you may conform to the tax year, which is the same for everyone, running from 6 April of one year to 5 April of the next.

When this book was being prepared the Inland Revenue was asked – as were other sources from which current data was required – if there was any information to which it was recommended that special emphasis might be usefully made. The reply was: 'Our experience suggests that particular attention should be drawn to the rather unusual assessing basis periods for Schedule D – especially in the opening and closing years.'

The Income Tax Year is usually referred to by identifying the two years involved in it. Thus the Income Tax Year beginning 6 April 1978 and ending 5 April 1979 is referred to as 'Income Tax Year 1978-79'. The general rule is that the assessment for an Income Tax Year is based on the profits of the twelve months' trading during the *previous* Income Tax

Year. This means that if accounts are regularly made up to 31 March, then the assessment for the Income Tax Year 1978-79 will be based on the twelve months' account ending in the Income Tax Year 1977-78 – in other words the twelve months' income between 6 April 1977 and 5 April 1978.

Special provisions apply when a business is begun, and also when it ends, although this book is not concerned with cessation of self-employment. For the first Income Tax Year – that is the year ending on the first 5 April after the start of the business – the assessment is based on the profits made from the commencement of business until 5 April. If the first accounts are made up to a later date, then a proportion is taken. For the second Income Tax Year, the assessment is made on the profits of the first full twelve months of trading. For the third Income Tax Year, the assessment is based on the profits of the twelve months ending on the usual accounting date in the preceding Tax Year. If no year fits this description, then the assessment is based on the profits of the first twelve months' trading.

The Inland Revenue give two examples to show how this works. They are quoted here in full.

Example 1
A trade begins on 6 October 1975 and the trader decides to make up accounts annually to 5 October. The Income Tax profits for the year ending 5 October 1976 are £4,000, for the year ending 5 October 1977 £4,800 and for the year ending 5 October 1978 £4,400. The assessments are:

1975-76 (based on six months to 5 April 1976) 6/12 x 4,000 =	£2,000
1976-77 (based on first twelve months' trading)	£4,000
1977-78 (based on year ending 5 October 1976)	£4,000
1978-79 (based on year ending 5 October 1977)	£4,800
1979-80 (based on year ending 5 October 1978)	£4,400

A taxpayer may choose to have the assessments for the second and third years of assessment (but not one only of those years) based upon the profits made in those years. Such a claim is normally beneficial if profits are lower in the second year of trading than in the first.

Example 2

A trade begins on 6 October 1975 and the trader decides to make up accounts annually to 5 October. The Income Tax profits for the year ending 5 October 1976 are £4,000, for the year ending 5 October 1977 £3,200 and for the year ending 5 October 1978 £4,400. Initially, the assessments for 1976-77 and 1977-78 are £4,000 each year, as in Example 1, but on application by the taxpayer (within seven years of the end of the second year of assessment) the assessments can be amended to:

1976-77 (based on year ending 5 April 1977)	
half of profits of year ending 5 October 1976	£2,000
plus half of profits of year ending 5 October 1977	£1,600
Total	£3,600
1977-78 (based on year ending 5 April 1978)	
half of profits of year ending 5 October 1977	£1,600
plus half of profit of year ending October 5 1978	£2,200
Total	£3,800

The assessment for 1978-79 is still based on the profits of the year ending 5 October 1977, so in this case the 1978-79 assessment is £3,200. The assessment for 1979-80, based on the profits of the year ending 5 October 1978, is £4,400, as in Example 1.

BOOKS AND RECORDS

When you contact your local Inspector of Taxes and tell him you are commencing business on your own account, he may wish to satisfy himself that this is true, and that you are not an employee merely working at home.

You will qualify for various expenses and allowances if you

are being paid a fee for services which you would not get if you were providing exactly the same services under a contract of employment. The Inspector must be satisfied that you are in control of a business, and not only entitled to the profits but the person responsible for any losses and thus entitled to any expenses and allowances for which there may be provision.

You will be required to give to the Inspector, annually, two different records:

Trading Account The first is a Trading Account, detailed as a Profit and Loss Account which summarizes the year's trading transactions. This is a digest of all business income received, and all business expenses incurred.

Balance Sheet The second is a Balance Sheet, which shows the 'assets' of the business and its liabilities at the beginning of the accountancy year and again at the end of it.

You can draw these accounts up yourself, or you can engage an accountant to present them for you. Either way only you can supply the information required. In either case it is essential to keep full and accurate records of all income and expenditure from the day the business begins. This is in your own interest.

If you cannot give the Inspector, either directly or through the accountant, an accurate and proveable statement of your profits, then the profits will be estimated by the Inspector of Taxes. The Inland Revenue's estimation is likely to be higher than one based on correct records. After the receipt of an estimated assessment from the Inland Revenue the onus is then on the taxpayer to prove that it is incorrect.

The kind of records you keep will depend very much on the nature of the business, but it is important to remember that it is essential to keep a record of any money, in cash, cheques or goods, that you take from the business to meet private expenditure or for personal use. The following chapter will deal specifically with the problems of book-keeping.

In small businesses, especially service businesses, where stock is not involved and where goods or services are paid for at the time, at the end of the accounting year the difference between business payments out and business takings represents the profit.

Where stock is involved, a stock-taking is necessary at the end of the accountancy year so that the increase or decrease of the value of the stock held may be taken into account, and can be shown as a gain or loss. Consumable goods – for example, stationery or fuel – are valued for stock-keeping purposes at the prices they cost you. Stock for resale, or as raw material for production, is valued at the cost to you, or at the net sale price anticipated if this happens to be lower than the cost, or at a lower figure if the current cost of the goods in the market in which they were purchased is now less than the cost at the time when they were bought.

A current record should be available at all times so that you always know how much is owing to you from customers and clients who have still to pay for goods or services they have had from you (your debtors) and how much you yourself owe for goods or services obtained for business purposes on credit (your creditors). Apart from the obvious need to have this information available at any time, the figures are necessary at the accountancy date to produce the Profit and Loss Account, and to arrive at the true profit figure for the business.

All documentation which provides evidence against which your figures may afterwards be checked should be kept – bank statements, paying in books, receipts and so on. Similar evidence relating to your private financial affairs should also be retained. If you are working from home, telephone, electricity, gas, fuel and rates bills and receipts should be kept. If you use your private car partly for business purposes a record of mileage made on business journeys should be kept.

CAPITAL ALLOWANCES

A distinction is drawn between 'capital' expenditure and 'revenue' expenditure.

Expenditure is categorized as 'capital' when it is spent on something which has a continuing value after the tax year in which it is bought. Examples are buildings, equipment and vehicles, and their replacements. Capital expenditure is expenditure on assets acquired and retained for the purpose of earning income.

Revenue expenditure, on the other hand, covers recurring expenses – accountancy fees, wages, rent, rates and repairs.

The Inland Revenue's booklet CA 1 covers capital allowances on plant, and CA 2 covers allowances on buildings.

The entire cost of any new plant and machinery may now be fully relieved in the year of acquisition or replacement. This full first-year allowance is not, however, available for expenditure on ordinary motor cars, unless they are for short-term hire (less than thirty days) or for the carriage of the general public, as in the case of car hire firms, taxi and minicab owners. First year allowance is, however, available on cars of a type constructed primarily for carrying goods. Since the use-value of equipment is spread over a number of years it may be advantageous similarly to spread the allowance.

In this case it is possible to claim no allowance during the year of purchase but to preserve a full future annual 'writing-down' allowance, usually given at 25%. Alternatively a 'restricted' allowance may be claimed during the first year. What is important to understand about a writing-down allowance is that it is not, in each year, a percentage related to the original cost, but a percentage related to whatever remains as the reduced balance of 'unrelieved' expenditure. For example, if £5,500 is spent on equipment in one year, a restricted allowance may be claimed of £2,000. This will leave an 'unrelieved' balance of £3,500. In the second year the writing-down allowance will be 25% not of £5,500, but of £3,500 – £875, leaving an unrelieved balance of £2,625.

Meanwhile the business may, in each or any year, acquire other new or replacement equipment, creating a capital allowances 'pool' figure, which covers all the equipment and machinery involved and not separate, individual items.

The importance of this to readers of this book is that if an established business is being bought, the capital allowance position of the business may be an asset acquired with the business. On the other hand, if any equipment involved in the business has been originally acquired (since 1972 when this become permissible) against a full first-year allowance, a very different assessment of the value of the business may be made.

In the case of motor cars, except where these are for short-term hire or for public carriage work, only the writing-down allowance of 25% is given, with a maximum figure. This is £2,000 for the first or any subsequent year for a car costing £5,000 or more bought after 12 June 1979; £1,250 for cars bought between 7 April 1976 and 11 June 1979; and £1,000 for cars bought before 6 April 1976.

Where a car is used partly for business and partly for private use, only a percentage of the allowance is made, and the figure has to be agreed with the Inspector of Taxes.

In the case of car-leasing each case is considered by the Revenue separately. When motor vehicles are leased (i.e. hired, often with an option to purchase at the end of the contract) the hire cost is allowable against revenue (*not* on capital allowances) with a proportion added back for private use (as director's benefit on limited companies) with separate treatment if acquired by the lessee at less than market value on termination of the contract.

Allowances are also made for the construction of industrial buildings – but not of shops or offices. The present initial allowance is 50%, and the present writing-down allowance is 4%. However, in this case the writing-down allowance is not a percentage of the reducing unrelieved expenditure, but of the original construction cost. This means that all the relief is exhausted in a period of twelve and a half years.

BUSINESS EXPENDITURE

The term 'business expenditure' is to be interpreted literally. The only expenses that can be deducted in arriving at the profits for tax are true and necessary business expenses. And these do not generally include the entertainment of business clients, except in cases where export business results – for example, overseas business clients. They may, however, include the cost of parties given by an employer to his own employees.

They include clothing – where this is uniform or protective clothing, and the condition is therefore met that the expense is incurred for something 'wholly and exclusively' needed for the work. On the other hand a professional television personality could claim the cost of a suit or a dress especially bought for a professional appearance, even though it might subsequently be worn on private occasions. The same personality, however, could not make a similar claim for everyday clothing on the argument that it was sometimes worn for television appearances.

The 'wholly and exclusively' rule is concerned with the true motive for expenditure. If an expense would have been incurred anyway, the fact that it has an incidental business value does not mean that the expense can be claimed. On the other hand, provided an expense is incurred solely for business purposes there is no risk of it being disallowed on the ground that incidental personal pleasures have been gained.

This means that if you make a journey to visit a client, you do not risk having your travelling expenses disallowed because you take the opportunity to visit a friend or relative living nearby. On the other hand you cannot put the expenses of a private visit to the friend or relative down to business simply by making a visit to a potential business client while you are in the district.

These situations of 'dual purpose' are inevitably in the grey area of interpretation and dispute. Clearly the Inland Revenue cannot investigate all the travelling expenses of every self-employed taxpayer. They can, however, microscopically investigate the travel of an individual taxpayer whose travelling – or any other – expenses seem unlikely to stand up to investigation.

The businessman who visits a conference being held in a holiday resort abroad, and who takes his wife with him, may find himself asked to show that there was no duality of purpose. It will not be sufficient for him to show evidence that he would not have gone to the resort if there had not been a conference there. He will have to show evidence that he would have gone to the resort and to the conference even if his wife could not have accompanied him, and even if there had been no 'leisure and pleasure' associated with the visit.

Travel from home to a regular place of business does not qualify as an expense. The argument is that such travel is undertaken to put the taxpayers in a position to undertake their work and that it is not essential to the work itself. On the other hand, if the business is conducted from home, then travel from the home to another place where a service is given, work is undertaken, or goods are sold, may be established as an expense. In some cases, where a person has a shop or office, it may even be possible to establish the home as being part of a 'dual base', the shop or office being run *from* the home, but *by* employees at business premises which have to be visited from time to time from the administrative home base.

USE OF PRIVATE RESIDENCE

The 'wholly and exclusively' ruling does not prevent apportionment of a total expenditure if it can be shown that some *part* of the expenditure is wholly and exclusively incurred for purposes of the business.

These 'partly allowable' expenses include rent, rates, lighting, heating and telephone facilities of premises used partly for business and partly for private habitation. The living premises behind or above the shop, the doctor and his private-house surgery, the freelance artist or writer, the home typist and all the other home-based business ventures qualify in this way. Also allowable are proportions of both the running costs and the hire-purchase charges of a car used for both business and pleasure. In every case agreement has to be reached with the Inspector of Taxes on the apportionment.

Self-employed people who wish to claim a business use of part of their home, and business expenses allowances on part of their relevant domestic bills, will have a better chance of persuading the Inspector to accept the claim and even to treat it in a generous way if they begin the business when they move into the house. If someone who has lived in a five-roomed house for a number of years suddenly decides to go into business on their own account and then seeks to claim a percentage of heating, lighting and telephone costs, they clearly do not have a very strong case unless they can show an increase in all these domestic bills over and above the normal inflationary increase. As for a claim for relief on rates and possibly rent on the grounds of accommodation used for business purposes, it may well be pointed out that they have no more accommodation than they ever had. Some Tax Inspectors may take a hard line with such claims.

There are other considerations, too. The local authority may increase the rates if a part-commercial use of the property is established, and thus any tax benefit set against a proportion of the rates would become lost. Again, if the Inland Revenue do accept that part of the house is used wholly and exclusively for business, part of the private-residence Capital Gains Tax exemption will be lost if and when the property is sold.

Private residences, may, of course, be transferred to company ownership, but in that case the whole of the Capital Gains exemption is sacrificed.

If the home is used as a base without any specific part of it being wholly and exclusively for business purposes, the proportion of running expenses that may be allowed will be lower, but the Capital Gains exemption will not be forfeit. This is probably the most advantageous arrangement, especially for a small-scale, part-time business venture.

SPOUSE'S WAGES AND PAYE

It may be argued that marriage is a civil contract of partnership. However a business partnership, from the point of view of tax law, is not automatically assumed by the Inland Revenue and has to be established as would be any other partnership, either orally or by Deed.

The role of a wife in connection with her husband's

business, or that of a husband in connection with a business owned by his wife, is more usually and advantageously that of an employee. The following conditions are described in terms of a wife assisting her husband in his business, but they apply equally to the reverse situation, except where stated.

A businessman may employ his wife in his business, whether the business is full-time or part-time, is operated from the home or from business premises. Her wages are an allowable expense, providing he pays her no more for the services than he would pay someone else for doing the same work – and provided he does pay her. A book is not enough.

She is treated as any other employee. If your wife's wage exceeds the appropriate limit, as her employer you must operate a PAYE deduction on her account. And if you become responsible for deducting PAYE – whether on your wife's wages or those of any other employee – you should ask your local Inspector of Taxes for a copy of the Employer's Guide to PAYE and the appropriate PAYE forms.

You will also be required to be responsible for National Insurance contributions for your wife, deducting her part of the contribution from the wage you pay her. In this connection you need to obtain leaflets P7 and NP15 from the local office of the Department of Health and Social Security.

It is obviously advantageous to employ your wife or husband in a capacity that justifies paying her or him a wage which will absorb their additional earned income allowance, which is currently a maximum of £1,375. (This allowance can only be claimed by the husband as, if the couple are taxed jointly, it is the husband who, by law, must fill in the Tax Return.)

Because of interaction with National Insurance contributions, it is currently advantageous to limit your wife's wage to £1,014 p.a., unless she is over the age of sixty.

It is beyond this amount that PAYE deductions become involved. National Insurance contributions are involved up to the wife's pensionable age of sixty, or up to the husband's pensionable age of sixty-five.

The full allowance of £1,165 may only be claimed if the wife's wage is at least that amount, and the lesser sum is taken if her wage is lower than this limit. There are also certain exclusions. These are any pension or other sum arising by reason of the husband's employment, any retirement pension or other National Insurance benefit except a retirement pension payable to her by reason of her own contribution, or a mobility allowance paid to her. The wage paid to the wife must be entered on the husband's Tax Return as her income, unless the husband and wife elect to be taxed separately. This is a situation which may arise where a husband and wife are jointly self-employed in a really profitable business. If the wife's involvement in the business is that of full partner it may be advantageous for her income from the business to be taxed as if she were a single woman with no other income. In this case the husband will also be entitled only to a single person's allowance, and the wife's earned income allowance will not be given.

An election for separate taxation does not, however, alter the treatment of the wife's *unearned* income, which continues to be assessed with her husband's total income. She therefore becomes responsible for paying tax on her earned income while he is responsible for paying the tax on her unearned income. The responsibility of returning details of the wife's earnings remains with the husband.

An election for separate taxation has to be made not earlier than six months before the end of the relevant tax year and not later than twelve months after the end of it. Whether this arrangement is worth making will normally depend upon the saving on high rates of tax outweighing the reduction in personal allowance and the loss of the wife's earned income allowance. Normally it is a matter in which the taxpayer must depend upon the accountant to recommend it if and when it becomes advantageous.

PARTNERSHIPS
A single assessment of income tax is made in the case of

partnerships, and each partner may be held fully responsible for the payment of the total tax. If a sole trader takes in a partner, or if any change in the structure of a partnership occurs, the business is considered for taxation purposes to have ceased at the time of the change and then to have recommenced, although there are provisions for partnership assessments to be treated on a continuing basis.

ASSESSMENTS, APPEALS AND PAYMENTS OF TAX

If your first accountancy year ends before your first Income Tax Return to show self-employment income is due to be made, then a copy of the accounts should be sent to the Inspector in advance of the Return. Otherwise, if possible, the accounts should be sent with the Return.

If your first accounts are prepared for the first twelve months of self-employment, they should be sent to the Inspector as soon as they are available. Normally no assessments will be made until after you have completed twelve months trading, but you may then receive two assessments, covering the first two Income Tax Years.

The tax on profits of a business is usually payable in two equal instalments, on 1 January and 1 July. If, when your business starts, you have two assessments at the same time, you have to be prepared to pay the tax on the whole of the first year – which would of course relate to a part year's income – within thirty days of the issue of the assessment. Payment of the first half of the second year's tax would be due on the following 1 January. If you fail to make a Return with a copy of your accounts in reasonable time, or if the Inspector is not satisfied that your accounts are correct, he will make his own estimate of the profits. You, or your accountant, then have thirty days in which to appeal against the assessment and to apply for postponement of payment. If for some special reason, such as sickness or bereavement, you need more than thirty days to prepare your appeal, you may apply to the Inspector to accept a late appeal.

Even though you have lodged an appeal the tax remains payable within thirty days of the issue of the assessment unless you apply for postponement of the amount you claim to have been overcharged. If the Inspector agrees with your figures then the tax that remains has then to be paid. If he does not agree then the General or Special Commissioners, an independent tribunal, will make the decision. Interest is chargeable on overdue tax. Two simple pieces of advice sum up this chapter.

1. Put aside, in special interest bearing funding, that part of all self-employment income that you anticipate may have to be paid in Income Tax. The purpose of the chapter has been to enable the reader to recognize what this is likely to be.
2. Employ an accountant to deal with the details – unless, of course, the self-employment you are proposing to take up *is* that of an accountancy service.

5: Keeping books, records and accounts

In the year 1495 a Franciscan monk, Lucas Pacioli, published a book, *De Computis et Scripturis*. This is the first known treatise on the subject of keeping account books. It introduced a system known for centuries as the 'Italian Method' which eventually became generally called double-entry book-keeping.

The first Englishman to write on the subject was James Peele, whose *How to keep a Perfect Accompte of Debitour and Creditour* was published in 1553. Since then there has been a continuous flow of books undertaking to make book-keeping and accountancy a 'do it yourself' accomplishment, simple enough for everyone to understand and easy enough for anyone to undertake.

Such, however, is the science of accountancy, by which the financial histories of businesses are written in figures, that it takes longer for accountants to qualify for the professional letters after their names than it may do for university undergraduates to gain their degrees. And in these days of complex accounting machines and sophisticated electronic computers this book will make no claim to make the services of a professional accountant unnecessary to every reader.

This does not mean that there could be any reader, embarking upon self-employment, who does not need to have a basic understanding of business book-keeping and an awareness of the essential nature of properly kept records.

Books and records must be kept, from the beginning of any business, from which any information, required by anyone, may be extracted and digested at any time. It must be possible to give the accountant a complete picture of the year's business and to be able to answer any question he may have or explain any figure he questions. The Inspector of Inland Revenue is not only equally demanding sometimes in his insistence upon detail but if the books and records are inadequate then he will substitute his estimates for the answers the taxpayer cannot supply. Understandably he will usually suspect attempted tax evasion rather than incompetent record keeping, and his margin of error will not be in the taxpayer's favour.

The Customs and Excise, if there is VAT registration, require their information every quarter. Proper business records may be essential in the seeking of any financial support from the bank manager or any other source. They will be required by business transfer agents, solicitors and potential purchasers if eventually the business comes to be sold. The value of the 'goodwill' and, therefore, the selling price, will depend largely on records that give a picture not only of the current state of the business but also give a quickly understandable picture of the relevant period of its trading history.

How much any individual reader may need to know from this book about book-keeping and accountancy will depend upon the nature of his or her self-employment and the circumstances under which he or she is commencing it.

The fact that no qualifications are necessary in the United Kingdom to practise accountancy means that the accounts sole traders or freelancers may themselves prepare, if they are adequate and understandable, will be acceptable to the Inland Revenue or to the Customs and Excise. It does not mean that the reader requires a crash course in accountancy.

The employee who takes on a little spare-time or freelance work to make some extra money will be able to get by with the simplest of commonsense records. A reader acquiring a shop or any other ready-made business will be taking over all the books of a ready-made book-keeping system and these will provide a pattern to follow. And those readers whose new businesses have complex accountancy problems – the readers possibly acquiring or setting up limited companies – will already have the services of a professional accountant or they would not be making such undertakings.

Let us look at the subject in a practical way, therefore.

SIMPLE PART-TIME SELF-EMPLOYMENT BOOK-KEEPING

Anyone commencing small scale, part-time self-employment may need to keep nothing more than an all-purpose book of record, used like a diary, in which receipts and payments are entered as they occur. Such an account book must, of course, be supported by all the available evidence. Specifically a receipts and payments book must record clear particulars of every separate payment of money received from a customer or client for goods or services supplied. It must show, in the same way, details of money spent on business purchases or expenses incurred for business purposes.

The supporting evidence should be filed under appropriate subject headings.

Filing system A good accounts filing system is possibly more important in the case of a small part-time business than an orthodox book-keeping system. If errors are suspected or found in your accountancy, they may be disproved or corrected if the relevant documentary evidence – a receipt, invoice, certificate or statement – has been kept and filed where it can be found. If your book-keeping is found, in retrospect, to be inadequate, or if there are gaps in it, the accounts may be built up later from filed evidence.

However simple the book-keeping may be at the beginning of part-time self-employment, the filing system should be comprehensive and intelligently organized. Filing folders should relate to the calendar year. A basic filing system requires a minimum of six folders:

1. Business bills and, if they are separate documents, the related receipts stapled to them. (Use staples rather than paper clips for such purposes.)

2. Invoices with related payment statements (or dates and details of payments) stapled to them.
3. Used cheque books, with filled in stubs, the dates of period of use marked on the covers; used paying-in books, similarly reference dated for period of use; bank statements, entries annotated and categorized at the time of issue from cheque book and paying-in book details.
4. Employers' PAYE salary or wage slips.
5. Domestic expense bills and receipts relating to matters in which there could be a claim for business allowance proportionment – telephone, rates, fuel or other heating and power bills, car expenses.
6. Certificates issued with any investment dividends or interest payments from building societies, local authority bonds, detailing tax deducted at source.

However small the self-employment operation, because it is taxed separately, and at a different time, and because it is subject to allowances and expenses that are related only to its income and expenditure, the principle to be followed in your book-keeping is that there must be a clear-cut, recognizable line separating it from other sources of income which are separately taxed, on a different basis and at a different time.

Records must show if money is drawn from the business for personal use, and if money is put into the business 'capital fund' – in other words if you use some of your income from other sources, or your savings, to buy things needed for the self-employment business.

Sensibly, although not essentially, the smallest of business operations should have its own bank account – possibly a No. 2 account being opened for it.

Bank statements showing transfers of money from the No. 2 account to the No. 1 account will then provide an authenticated record of money being taken from the business as personal income from it, while transfers the other way round will record capital being introduced into the business, differentiating it from earnings of the business.

Readers commencing limited part-time or full-time self-employment have two important points to remember in evolving a simple system of book-keeping and filing that will meet their immediate requirements.
1. If the business establishes itself and expands, then eventually the services of a professional accountant will be needed. His immediate value may largely depend upon there being properly kept and understandable books and records from the date of the first business expense incurred or the first income received, whichever was the earlier.
2. Because income earned and expenses incurred in self-employment are treated both by the Inland Revenue and by the Department of National Health and Social Security in a different way from income earned in employment, it is a requirement of book-keeping and records to keep the two financial operations distinct and separate from the commencement of business. Remember, in this connection, that your own memory of transactions and details cannot be put on file.

The simplest of receipts and payments book-keeping might be that of someone doing a limited amount of copy typing at home. Jane Doe, for example, undertakes typing at home for a secretarial agency and also does some copy typing for a couple of local writers, having advertised her available service in the local weekly newspaper. A monthly excerpt from her accounts book might read like this:

Sample page of Jane Doe's receipts and payments book

Date	Client	Payment for	Invoice No.	Payments in	Reserve for tax fund	Purchases	Supplier	Amount
Carried forward (from December)				£1,248.73	£388.00			£82.20
Jan. 1	Abbey National	Half-yearly dividend		£16.20				
Jan. 9	Hometype Agency	Legal documents	109	£11.50	£4.00			
Jan. 15						Typewriter ribbon and paper	Becsupply Ltd.	£9.24
Jan. 16	John Righter	Book MS	103	£56.00	£16.00			
Jan. 19	Hometype Agency	Company report	110	£6.00	£2.00			
Jan. 22						Small ad.	Weekly Chronicle	£1.50
Jan. 25	R. E. Porter	Feature article	114	£4.50	£1.00			
Carry forward (to February)				£1,342.93	£411.00			£92.94

Jane Doe would also keep a separate invoice book, always submitting her invoice with finished work when it was delivered or collected. The excerpt relevant to her January accounts book might read like this:

Sample page from Jane Doe's invoice book

Date	Invoice	Client	Work	Charge	Paid
Nov. 30	103	John Righter	Book MS	£56.00	Jan. 16
Nov. 30	104	Hometype	Appeal letters	£8.50	Dec. 7
Dec. 8	105	Hometype	Legal documents	£3.20	Dec. 14
Dec. 13	106	Hometype	Translation copy	£9.00	Dec. 21
Dec. 19	107	R. E. Porter	Short story	£3.00	Dec. 19
Dec. 21	108	Hometype	Author's copy work	£5.00	Dec. 29
Dec. 29	109	Hometype	Legal documents	£11.50	Jan. 9
1979					
Jan. 12	110	Hometype	Company report	£6.00	Jan. 19
Jan. 14	111	John Righter	Book index	£8.00	
Jan. 16	112	Hometype	Legal documents	£4.00	
Jan. 18	113	Hometype	Report	£5.00	
Jan. 25	114	R. E. Porter	Feature article	£4.50	Jan. 25

These two simple books, in Jane Doe's case, give her a complete record of her part-time work, from which she has a gross turnover of between £1,600 and £1,700 a year. Her invoice book shows her at any time how much money she is still owed for work she has done, and which has been delivered and collected. Her accounts book records all the necessary details of every item of income and of expenditure directly belonging to her business. The monthly totals tell her what her gross income has been so far for the year. It tells her what her direct business expenses have been. It records the amount reserved for her Income Tax fund.

Jane Doe keeps her self-employment Income Tax fund in a building society 'paid up shares' account, where it earns interest. The first entry in her accounts book for the year is therefore the end-of-year interest in this account. As it is taxed at source none of it has to be shown in the tax fund column.

Jane takes one-third of every payment for work she does and puts it immediately into the building society account. She rounds the figure upwards to the nearest £1 with the intention of achieving a genuine savings fund by both over-estimating the tax she will eventually pay and overpaying on that over-estimation.

However, when the expenses side of her accounts book has an entry, she deducts this amount from the next payment in and estimates her tax fund deduction from the balance. Thus, on 15 January she spent £9.25 on a typewriter ribbon, typing paper and other office sundries listed on the bill filed away. The following day her late-paying client, John Righter, paid her the £56 which had been owing to her since 30 November. She deducted the £9.25 from this to arrive at the sum from which to deduct the one-third for her 'tax fund' building society account. The balance being £46.76, she 'rounded up' the one-third of this from £15.58 to £16.

BASIC BOOK-KEEPING FOR A SMALL TRADER

The object of any book-keeping system should be to reduce

clerical work to a minimum and yet to have records that can produce any information that may be required easily, quickly and at any time. A basic system for a small trader, who has no employees and who is not involved in VAT, is one that takes full advantage of the fact that the bank does all the book-keeping for payments in and out.

Whatever his business, the trader has two matters to deal with:
1. Monies received from customers.
2. Payments made to suppliers and expenses incurred.

An accountant is likely to recommend and require such a businessman to keep four separate categories of records:
1. A cash book
2. A bank record book
3. Two arch files for customer accounts
4. Two arch files for suppliers and expenses accounts.

1. The cash book On the left hand page, or 'debit' side, is entered:
a All cash received. That is: all cash payments made by customers and any cash withdrawn from the bank.
b All cheques received from customers.
On the right hand page, or 'credit' side, is entered:
a All cash paid into the bank.
b All cash (as opposed to cheque) payments made to suppliers or for other expenses.

2. The bank record book This is simply a record of payments into the bank account and cheques drawn against the account, analysing and detailing them for full future reference. Retained cheque book stubs matched against quarterly bank statements produce the same kind of result, but may be inadequate and may lead to errors.

When annual accounts are being prepared, a bank statement may show that cheque No. 863507, for a sum of £19, passed through the account on 15 April a year earlier. But the entry, as such, is likely to be meaningless after the passage of time. Who was paid the £19, and for what reason?

The cheque book stub may provide the additional

information that the payment was to Richard Roe. But, unless Richard Roe is a regular customer, after a lapse of time it may be impossible to remember who he was, and for what he was paid – whether for stock for resale, consumable goods, for a purchase to be categorized as revenue expenditure or one to be categorized as capital expenditure. Such details need to be recorded at the time of the transaction.

The balance in the bank record book should be checked against the bank's quarterly statements and should, when bank charges have been entered, produce the same figure.

3. Customer bills Two arch files, sometimes known as 'transfer cases', are recommended for these records. An arch file is a loose-leaf file, with twin, lever-operated metal-rod arches onto which documents, having had appropriately spaced holes punched into left hand margins, may be filed.

The first of the two files is labelled 'Customers Bills – Unpaid', the second 'Customers Bills – Paid'.

When bills are to be sent to customers they should be prepared in triplicate. The top copy goes to the customer. One carbon copy goes into the correspondence files. The second carbon copy is filed in the 'Unpaid' arch file. When the customer pays, this copy is taken from the 'Unpaid' file and transferred to the 'Paid' file.

4. Suppliers, bills and expenses The second pair of arch files are labelled respectively: 'Bills – Unpaid' and 'Bills – Paid'.

As bills from suppliers, or for expenses, are received they are filed in the first of this pair of files. When they are paid, they are transferred to the second file. The 'Unpaid' files of each pair will show at any time how much money is owing to the business and is owed by it.

DOUBLE-ENTRY BOOK-KEEPING

The simple system of receipts and payments book-keeping is known as single-entry book-keeping. It may be adapted and expanded to cover the needs of most self-employment ventures. Indeed it is probably safe to say that if more than this is needed, then the reader will need the services of an accountant and not a book on accountancy – in which case the accountant will either take the single-entry book-keeping records and produce from them the Profit and Loss Account and the Balance Sheet required from him by the Inland Revenue, or will say what other or different kinds of records the particular business needs to simplify his work and thereby to reduce his charges.

Most small self-employment businesses do not use double-entry book-keeping. Most small shopkeepers, if they are asked, will admit that they do not understand the system and if they do, they will say that they do not have the time needed to operate it.

Nevertheless if the reader goes to his local library and consults any books on accountancy and book-keeping, he is immediately going to be confronted with double-entry book-keeping and may falsely assume that it is necessary and is universally used. However, a general understanding of the system, upon which business practice is based, is worth having.

The principle of double-entry book-keeping is a very simple one. If you buy something, then there is a deduction from your capital or cash in hand which is balanced out by an addition to your stock or assets. On the other hand, if you sell something, then your capital or cash is increased while your stock or assets diminish.

Double-entry book-keeping recognizes that every business transaction must have these two aspects to it, regardless of whether the exchange is favourable or not, and that both aspects of the transaction must be separately entered in such a way that the one balances the other. Debits (Dr.) are always entered on the left hand page of an account and Credits (Cr.) are always entered on the right hand page. The rule is that the receiver is always debited while the giver is always credited.

To anyone unfamiliar with book-keeping and accountancy it is this rule that often makes double-entry book-keeping difficult to understand. A business bank account in-payment, for instance, is shown as a debit not a credit entry. The reason for this is quite logical. If you have just paid £100 into your bank account, naturally you think of yourself as being 'in credit' for that amount at the bank. So, indeed, you are – in the bank's books. But in your own books, if you are using the double-entry book-keeping system, the bank has to be shown as owing you £100, and therefore the figure is entered on the debit side of your ledger.

From an accountancy point of view, double-entry book-keeping has a number of advantages over the single-entry system. Because every debit entry has, somewhere in the books, a corresponding credit entry, at any one time the total debits *must* equal the total credits. This fact allows a quick test of the accuracy and correctness of the book-keeping. It allows the compilation of a Profit and Loss Account and a Business Balance Sheet to be made quickly and accurately. It minimizes any risk there may be of fraud or of its concealment. And because it records not only the 'personal' transactions of receipts and purchases with debtors and creditors but also the impersonal things like fittings, fixtures and their depreciation as assets, it provides a much more accurate picture of the true state of the business. This may be very different from the picture given by a comparison between gross turnover and the cost of purchases during the period related to the turnover.

Whether a business uses the single-entry system of book-keeping or the double-entry system depends upon the kind of business. In either case the exact nature of the books to be kept will again vary between one business and another.

The simple test for the individual reader about the system he will use in his new self-employment business is this. If you can handle your accounts and deal with the Inland Revenue and the Customs and Excise yourself, then you need nothing more complicated than a single-entry ledger recording details of receipts and purchases. If you recognize the need for the services of an accountant, let him tell you what books and records *he* wants you to keep, and how he wants them to be kept.

6: *VAT*

It is fanciful speculation but, if by revision and reprints this book continued to be in publication over a sufficient number of years, a time might eventually arise when this chapter would become Chapter 4, VAT having completely replaced Income Tax. The French, who started this kind of 'turnover tax' in 1954 have travelled quite a long way towards such a situation. The fiscal policies of the present (Tory) UK government are recognizably directed along these lines. And it makes sense. VAT provides a much more efficient tax net than Income Tax.

If the reader is going to have to get to grips with the problems of Value Added Taxation, understanding begins with knowing what problems lie behind the tax. And problems there are, because VAT turns almost all the self-employed into members of an army of tax collectors.

When the European Economic Community was formed, the idea was to create a vast international trading and business market in which each member nation's manufacturers, producers, traders and businesses offering services could operate throughout the whole community of nations with no more hindrances than they encountered when operating in the smaller market of their own country. The elimination of 'effects and factors likely to distort or disturb competition' was a main issue. The existence of completely different tax systems in the various member countries was – and still remains – a major cause of these 'distortions' in the conditions of competition. The answer was to introduce a common 'turnover tax' of the kind the French were operating. This would be at least a beginning of the harmonizing of the different national tax systems.

This is how Value Added Tax came into being. This is why, having joined the EEC on 1 January 1973, the United Kingdom introduced VAT on the following 1 April. And this is why VAT is operated by the Customs and Excise and not by the Inland Revenue. Fundamentally it is an international rather than an internal taxation system.

National taxation systems develop from the economic, social and religious history of the nations concerned. Their roots go deep into the distant past with the consequence that they are complex and difficult to understand. History can never be revised and only the most dramatic situations make it possible to sweep its consequences aside and to make a fresh start. The entry of the UK into the EEC and the consequential introduction of VAT offered such an opportunity to those framing the regulations for the new tax and setting up its administrative organization. That chance was lost.

A complicated, time-wasting, ill-planned system was launched which now requires some thirty-six officially issued Customs and Excise booklets to attempt to explain it in the painful terminology of bureaucracy – a system which has caused a quite unjustifiable amount of extra work and an incalculable amount of stress and worry to many small traders.

None of this, it must be added at once, is the fault of any of the VAT administrators with whom the readers of this book may have to deal. They, too, are the victims. They, indeed, are the people upon whom the retailer, for example, may best rely for advice when he begins business as to which of nine VAT 'Special Schemes for Retailers' is most suitable for his kind of business and how, then, to operate it.

We have been saddled with VAT as it is, and this chapter is therefore concerned with how the tax, and its administration, may affect those who, by their decision to become self-employed, become *immediately* concerned with Value Added

Tax considerations the moment they have made that decision. And everybody who goes into business on his own account, on whatever scale, even if it is a matter of occasional freelance work, should consider VAT registration.

The reader who has been told that 'you don't *have* to register to pay VAT if your taxable turnover is under £13,500 a year' and who has no anticipation of such a business income, now or ever, may be making a very expensive mistake by being delighted to be 'off the hook'.

There are circumstances in which those entering the field of self-employment should loudly insist on their *right* to register for and to collect Value Added Tax. There are even circumstances in which, although no Value Added Tax will ever be payable, VAT registration should be made from the first day of self-employment.

VAT registration may be a nuisance, but it need never involve a financial penalty or loss of income to those in business. On the contrary, where it relates to business transactions it should *always* represent a 'pay-back'.

HOW VAT WORKS

VAT is a tax imposed upon most goods and services. The collectors of the tax are :
1. The producers
2. The manufacturers
3. The wholesalers
4. The retailers
5. The suppliers of services

Each collector of the tax 'passes the buck' down the line until it ends up in the lap of the public (the consumer) as part of the purchase or of the charge for a service.

In theory, the tax works like this :
1. The producer (A) sells £1,000 worth of natural raw material to a manufacturer. The raw material is subject to a current VAT rating of 15%. Because his total annual taxable turnover exceeds £13,500, A is VAT registered. He must therefore charge the manufacturer an additional £150 as Value Added

Tax. He does so and, having collected the £150, passes it on to Customs and Excise.

2. The manufacturer (B) turns the raw material into manufactured goods which he then sells to a wholesaler. His total annual taxable turnover also exceeds £13,500 so he too is VAT registered. Whatever his total invoiced charge is to the wholesaler, it includes the £150 VAT he has paid to A. As he is VAT registered he is entitled to recover this £150 because it was paid on raw materials needed for his business. And he has now recovered it from the wholesaler.

3. The wholesaler (C) sells the manufactured goods to a retailer. His taxable turnover exceeds £13,500 a year, he is VAT registered and at whatever new price he sells the goods to the retailer the 15% VAT he adds to the price includes the original £150. He recovers this money from the retailer.

4. The retailer (D) sells the goods to the public. If D's annual taxable turnover exceeds £13,500, he too will be VAT registered and he must add 15% VAT to the price at which he sells his goods. In the total VAT he accumulates from the sale of all these particular goods will be included the original £150 which A collected from B and then paid to the Customs and Excise. Unless any of the customers are themselves VAT registered and making the purchase for business use, there the process ends, with the consumer paying all the tax.

If D's annual taxable turnover does not exceed £13,500 and he is not registered for VAT then he is not allowed to charge his customers the extra 15% and he ends up paying the whole £150 himself.

5. E, the supplier of a service, may fit anywhere into the VAT taxation chain. The service he supplies may be given to a producer, manufacturer, wholesaler or retailer as a necessary business service, and the VAT on this is then passed on down the line. If the service has no business purpose it is given to a 'consumer' with whom the tax stops.

The conclusion to be reached from this story is very obvious. If, whatever your trade or profession, you are paying VAT on products, goods or services needed in connection with your gainful self-employment, then you should consider applying for voluntary VAT registration even if your taxable turnover is never likely to be high enough to make such registration obligatory. The theoretical example given, tracing a chain of taxation from an initiating producer through manufacturer, wholesaler, retailer and down to the eventual and ultimate taxpayer, the consumer, is not, of course, how the tax works or could work in practice.

To understand the reality consider our manufacturer, B. In making the goods he eventually sold to C, the wholesaler, B used other raw materials, on which he paid VAT. He also bought ready-made component parts, some from other manufacturers and some from wholesalers, paying VAT in each case. Mostly these purchases of raw materials and components went into stock, and he actually used different percentages of each in the particular batch of goods this example is examining.

Apart from the cost of the materials and components used in making these particular goods, he also has a production cost to estimate. Some aspects of this – used machinery, tools, equipment, stationery, telephone and professional services like advertising – had already been or would be increased by his own payments of VAT upon the goods and services involved. It would be clearly impossible in such a case to estimate the proportions of every related VAT payment and to produce a figure that could be added to the selling price of each item of manufacture in order to recover the correct amount of tax.

In practice, therefore, this is what happens:

At the end of the three months tax period in which he made his purchase from A of the basic raw materials, B prepares his VAT return. He finds that during these three months his total purchases of VAT-rated products, goods and services have cost him £6,000, plus £900 VAT. During the same tax-period he finds that he has sold £9,200 worth of manufactured goods on which he has charged, and collected, an extra £1,380 VAT. The tax he has to pay at the end of this tax quarter is, therefore:

Total tax due	
On 'outputs' (sales of manufactured goods) at the standard rate	£1,380.00
Tax deductible	
Deductible 'input' tax on purchase of goods and materials in UK ... £780.00	
Plant and equipment £112.50	
Telephone (on £50 bill) £7.50	
Total tax deductible £900.00	£900.00
Net tax due to Customs and Excise	£480.00

There are three points of importance to note here.

1. It may well be that at the end of this tax quarter B has not yet sold the manufactured goods to C. Nevertheless he has already recovered the £80 tax he paid A for the raw materials from which the goods are being made. Recovery of VAT paid out is always made within the three months tax period in which it has been paid. Indeed it may often happen that tax already collected for payment to the Customs and Excise at the end of the tax period will be available to meet tax that has to be paid out on products, goods or services required during the quarter.

2. Generally, unless the trader is dealing in zero-rated goods, there will always be a balance of tax to pay the Customs and Excise at the end of each quarter. This situation arises because that part of the price of goods that represents the seller's profit is also subject to VAT. This is tax which begins with the buyer and is, therefore, not tax that the seller has ever paid and is not subject to his recovery.

If we go back to our original theoretical example it is now possible, in the light of this profit consideration, to see why Value Added Taxation is so important to the Treasury.

A sells £1,000 worth of raw materials to manufacturer B, adding VAT at 15%	VAT £150.00
B sells manufactured goods to wholesaler C allowing himself a profit of 30% on which VAT of 15% is charged	£45.00
C sells the goods to the retailer D adding on a profit of 25%, on which VAT is charged at 15%	£48.75
D sells the goods to the public adding a 40% profit margin on the price they have actually cost him from C, on which VAT is charged	£97.50
Total VAT collected by Customs and Excise	£341.25

3. Failure to apply for VAT registration may be costly, and the 'taxable turnover' may be misleading.

Consider two cases of two men retiring on pension and deciding to supplement their pensions by gainful self-employment. The one buys a small 'corner shop' business and derives from it a net income before tax of only £2,000 a year. His sale of VAT-rated goods over the counter, however, represents a gross turnover of over £13,500 a year. He therefore has to register for VAT and discovers, as a consequence, how the Input-Output balancing-out works to his favour.

The other man provides a service. His taxable turnover of VAT-rated services is the same as his income from his services. He may therefore have a net income before tax of £8,000 a year, four times as much as the shopkeeper, yet not be required to register for VAT. Yet the total VAT he pays himself on goods and services he needs for his business could, during the course of the year, be a sum well worth recovering.

VAT RATINGS AND REGISTRATION

Registration for VAT is a legal requirement if your total taxable sales or services produce certain minimum turnover figures (as distinct from profit) during certain periods. Certain things are outside the scope of VAT – for example, wages and salaries, rent and rates – and others are exempt, for example, education, health, burial and cremation, postal services, land and property sales. All other goods sold and services supplied in the United Kingdom are generally subject to VAT rating.

VAT ratings may vary from time to time, but the ratings fall into two categories – zero-rated and positive-rated goods and services.

The zero-rated list may change from time to time. It currently includes food, books and newspapers, newspaper advertisements and news services, fuel and power, transport, drugs and medicines, charities, children's and certain other clothing and footwear. Although no VAT is actually paid on zero-rated items, zero-rate *is* a 'rate of tax'. Businesses dealing only in the sale of zero-rated goods or the supply of zero-rated services, must still register if their 'taxable turnover' is above the levels laid down. And such businesses, although they collect no VAT from their own customers for transfer to the Customs and Excise, may nevertheless claim back the VAT they themselves pay to suppliers in connection with their businesses. The typical example here is the butcher.

Positive rates of taxes, and the goods and services to which they apply, are liable to variation. Currently there is now one general rate of 15%.

Registration is required by law if, at the end of any calendar quarter (i.e. 31 March, 30 June, 30 September, 31 December) the total taxable turnover has exceeded £4,000 for that quarter. If the annual turnover anticipatable will be below £12,500, the 'deregistration' figure, point this out when making notification of your liability to register. Even if the £4,000 has not been reached or exceeded, if at any time there is reason to anticipate that the taxable turnover will exceed £13,500 during the next twelve months, then registration is required. These minimum figures may be changed from time to time.

Where there is a liability to register it is essential not to delay. You are required to account for and pay any tax due from the date when you first became liable and not from the date when you notify the Customs and Excise of your liability to be registered, or the date when you receive your Certificate of Registration. If you are late in making the notification, and in collecting the tax yourself, you will still be liable to pay the arrears of tax even if you have not charged it to your customers or clients – and you will not be able to claim credit for the VAT you yourself have paid out. Registration must be applied for within ten days of the end of the quarter in which it becomes necessary. Later notification may mean that the registration will be back-dated. If you fail to notify liability for registration you are liable to a penalty of £1,000 or, if greater, three times the amount of the tax evaded by the failure or contravention.

If you think you are liable for VAT registration, or wish to register before you are liable, because you are starting a new business, because you are dealing in zero-rated items, or because you are mainly exporting, your first move is to contact your local Customs and Excise VAT office. The address is listed in the local telephone directory (not the *Yellow Pages*). You require from them Form VAT 1, which is the Notification of Liability to be Registered for Value Added Tax, and incorporates an application for voluntary registration as a taxable person on grounds which have to be outlined in an accompanying letter. There is a separate Welsh version of this application form, Form VAT 20, obtainable from the Cardiff, Chester and Swansea Customs and Excise main VAT offices and at sub-offices in Wales.

The covering letter when you return the completed form should ask that the quarterly registration date should coincide with the end of your financial year, as a matter of convenience.

In the case of a partnership, Form VAT 2 is required.

In the case of a new business dealing in zero-rated goods or services, application may be made to be exempt from registration. In this case Form VAT 1 must still be completed and sent to the local Customs and Excise main office with a letter applying for exemption and explaining why it is required. If the application is approved the right to reclaim any VAT paid for business goods or services is, of course, sacrificed.

You should start keeping VAT records and begin charging VAT to your customers from the date when you first become aware that you are liable to register, and not wait until you receive your registration number. You must not show VAT on any invoice until you know the number, but should adjust your selling price to include VAT, explaining to your registered customers that a VAT tax invoice will be sent by you to them when you are given a VAT registration number.

Within four weeks of submitting Form VAT 1 the local VAT office will issue a Certificate of Registration and a VAT number. This will give you the effective date of registration and from that date you *must* start invoicing customers and clients giving details of the VAT charges, and your registration number. If your business involves giving quotations, these must show your VAT registration number and must specify whether quotations made include or exclude VAT. If the business involves issuing order forms, these must carry your VAT registration number.

From the date of registration you must issue invoices that conform to VAT requirements – and retain and file copies of them. These invoices must give your name, or business name if it is different, and the address from which the business is conducted. It must give the customer's name and address. It must have an identifying invoice serial number. It must be dated and show the 'Tax Point' date. There must be a description of the goods or services, the selling price, any rate of discount allowed, and the type of sale involved (i.e. sale, hire or hire-purchase). The total cost of the goods should be shown. VAT rate, and the amount applicable to each sale on the invoice must be shown. The total VAT charged must be given.

There are two points of importance to note here.

1. If there is, say, a discount for cash payment within an immediate period of time, then the VAT charged is calculated on the discounted charge. You are liable to pay the VAT charges you have invoiced during the quarter of the trading

VAT 95

whether you are paid by the customer or client during the period or not. If the customer or client sacrifices the discount by late payment, the VAT charge to the customer and your liability to the Customs and Excise are not increased.

2. The 'Tax Point' is a specific date. It may be the date of the issue of the invoice but it may otherwise be the date on which the customer received or took the goods, or the date on which a service to a client was completed. The Tax Point is whichever is the earlier of the two dates. You will find that the Customs and Excise are very specific about Tax Points because, by putting the date back, the taxpayer could move a transaction from one quarter into the succeeding quarter, and have the benefit of an improved cash position for up to three months.

The issue of invoices for zero-rated goods and services, and for supplies to customers who are not taxable, is optional.

In some businesses the transactions are such that tax invoices are not possible, or where invoices or bills could not give all the information normally required. The Customs and Excise may then approve less detailed records. Arrangements for shopkeepers are dealt with separately, later in this chapter.

In certain exceptional cases the Customs and Excise will approve what is known as self-billing arrangements. This means that the invoice is made out by the customer or client and not by the person collecting the tax and paying it to the Customs and Excise. The circumstances in which such arrangements may be used include situations where you cannot invoice because you do not know how much to invoice for – for example, if you are supplying a product to someone who subsequently pays you a royalty or syndication fee for the unpredictable use they may sell of 'published' material, over an equally unpredictable period of time. This situation applies especially to the work of recording artistes, artists and writers.

Besides sending off Form VAT 1 and becoming registered, the taxable person must thereafter:

1. Record his Outputs (sales of goods or services) and the VAT on them.

2. Issue tax invoices showing the VAT, when required.
3. Record his Inputs (business purchases of goods and services) and the VAT paid on them, retaining all bills.
4. Work out, for each tax period, the difference between his Output tax and his deductable Input tax, in order to complete his VAT return.
5. Keep records and accounts that are adequate. Records and accounts do not have to be kept in any special form, but if those being kept do not satisfy the requirements of the Customs and Excise they have the power to direct the taxable person to make such changes as they require so that they may check the completeness and accuracy of the returns. These records and accounts have to be kept for three years. Where a taxable person's business is subject to an independent audit, the audit has to cover the VAT accounts. The Customs and Excise are now sometimes requiring copies of annual accounts as submitted to the Inland Revenue so that these may be reconciled with their figures.
6. Keep a VAT Account. For each tax period a taxable person must summarize his records of Output tax (including tax on any goods applied to personal use), tax due but not paid on imported or warehoused goods, deductable Input tax, and tax adjustments affecting the amount due or the amount repayable by the Customs and Excise. These summaries must be entered in a special book, ledger opening, or file, known as the VAT Account – showing 'Tax Due' to the Customs and Excise, 'Tax Deductable' and the 'Net Amount' for payment or repayment

Again there is no requirement that a VAT Account must follow a particular pattern. It must however contain this information, to enable the taxable person to fill up his VAT returns and enable the Customs and Excise officer to check them.

After you have been registered, the registration forms are passed on to the computerized headquarters – HM Customs and Excise, VAT Central Unit, Alexander House, 21 Victoria Avenue, Southend-on-Sea, Essex SS99 1AA (Tel: Southend-on-Sea 48944).

VAT 97

It is this office that sends out the quarterly tax forms which have to be completed and returned with the tax due. The current, greatly simplified V A T Return form looks like this:

Return of Value Added Tax

For the period
".. ..... to. ..."
These dates must not be altered without the agreement of Customs and Excise.

For Official Use

Registration No.   Period No.

The person named here must complete the whole of this form (writing "none" where appropriate) in accordance with the instructions contained overleaf and return it in the enclosed envelope to the Controller, VAT Central Unit, HM Customs and Excise, 21 Victoria Ave., SOUTHEND-ON-SEA X, SS99 1AT.

not later than

The tax payable must be paid by the same date by remittance enclosed with this form or by National or Bank Giro.

WARNING
A return which is incomplete or qualified in any way (e.g. marked "Provisional") does not satisfy the legal requirements. Failure to make a return or to pay the full amount of tax payable by the due date is an offence.

	Account of tax payable or repayable		£	p
FOR OFFICIAL USE	TAX DUE in this period on OUTPUTS (sales, etc.)	1		
	Tax due on imported goods, goods from bonded warehouses and services received from abroad	2		
	Underdeclarations and/or underpayments of tax in previous periods notified in writing by Customs and Excise	3		
	Other underdeclarations made on previous returns	4		
	(Total of boxes 1, 2, 3 and 4) **TOTAL TAX DUE**	5		
	TAX DEDUCTIBLE being the credit claimed in this period for input tax allowable (on purchases, etc.)	6		
	Overdeclarations and/or overpayments of tax in previous periods notified in writing by Customs and Excise	7		
	Other overdeclarations made on previous returns	8		
	(Total of boxes 6, 7 and 8) **TOTAL TAX DEDUCTIBLE**	9		
	NET TAX PAYABLE OR REPAYABLE (Difference between boxes 5 & 9)	10		

Please tick the following boxes if "YES" is appropriate:
- Box 8 includes bad debt relief
- Box 11 includes exempt outputs
- Box 11 includes exports

Total values of Outputs and Inputs (excluding any Value Added Tax)

Outputs (sales, etc.)   11
Inputs (purchases, etc.) 12

Please tick ONE only of the following boxes:

If box 5 is greater than box 9: Payment by Giro ☐ Payment enclosed ☐

Special schemes for Retailers (Notice No. 727)
If you have used any of the schemes please tick the box(es) marked with the appropriate letter(s)

| A | B | C | D | E | F | G | H | J |

If box 9 is greater than box 5: Repayment due ☐

Declaration by the signatory to be completed by or on behalf of the person named above.

I, ... declare that the
(full name of signatory in BLOCK LETTERS)
information given in this return is true and complete.

Signed .... Date ....
(*Proprietor, partner, director, secretary, responsible officer, member of club or association, duly authorised person) *Delete as necessary.

FOR OFFICIAL USE

VAT 100   F.3790 (Oct. 1978)

Form V A T 100 reproduced above is Crown copyright and is printed by permission of H M Customs and Excise.

Correspondence about the periodic returns, payments and repayments are handled by the Central Unit, which also makes any repayments that may be due to a registered taxpayer. All other matters should be taken up with the local main VAT office of the Customs and Excise.

Shortly after registration a Customs and Excise Officer will make an appointment and visit you at your place of business. He will discuss your books and records, explain how to keep them as simply as possible, give you advice on how VAT affects you and generally help you with any problems you may have.

You should have your problems and questions ready for him. Where procedures are involved, or agreements about them are reached – for example self-billing arrangements – you should ask to have them confirmed in writing. If it is important that they should be on record, he will arrange this anyway.

Any changes to the information you have given on Form VAT 1 (change of business name, address, bank account, goods and services supplied, partnerships, change to status of a limited company, diversification or expansion of your business) has to be notified within twenty-one days.

From time to time you will receive further visits. Normally you will have prior notice of such visits, but not necessarily so.

RETAILER'S RECORDS

If you are considering starting or taking over a retailing business the invoicing rules on Outputs (sales) require special explanation and understanding. Since all the taxable goods a retailer sells represent stock on which he himself had to pay VAT when he acquired it, registration by any retailer must be regarded as automatic. In such businesses the only record of sales that you have to keep for your Outputs is a summary of each day's takings, differentiating the turnover into categorizations of positive VAT rating, zero-rating and exempt items.

For the purposes of VAT, the term retailer refers not only to a shopkeeper but to anyone supplying goods or services direct to the public without issuing invoices – unless the purchaser requests one. At least half of the business must be of this non-invoicing kind for it to be categorized as a retail business. In general, of course, the retailer is the shopkeeper, but the categorization includes restaurants, cafés and hotels.

The retailer's calculation of Outputs for VAT can be very complicated. It must show both cash and cheque takings after discounts have been made but before any expenses are paid. It has to show the face value of any trading stamps, offer coupons or tokens that are received. It has to include the cost, and the VAT, of any items taken from stock for personal use. It has to show deposits paid on goods. It has to show sales made against credit cards. It has to show discount sales made to another trader. It has to show the full retail value of goods or services accepted as 'payments in kind'. It has to show the retail value of goods sold on credit or hire-purchase even if payment is not received.

The record must also detail as deductions any refunds to customers, stamp charges made by trading stamp scheme companies, and cash exchange for trading stamps or coupons. All zero-rated sales and exempt sales have also to be recorded.

Sophisticated modern cash registers, which may cost the small shopkeeper around £1,000, are designed to produce categorized totals at the end of each day's trading. These records are acceptable to the Customs and Excise.

It is, of course, necessary that prices shown in shops shall be the total price payable and should already include VAT. The formula for calculating VAT that has already been included in the price of individual goods, or the total VAT due on sales of 15% VAT-rated goods during a day, is very simple. The price or the total is divided by twenty-three and the result is multiplied by three. This is a 'magic' formula worth remembering.

Thus if you sell an item in your shop for £1, the amount of VAT is 13.043478p! But the day's trading gives you a total turnover from which a round figure of VAT may be reached. Say the day's cash register takings of taxable sales are £247.23.

The Output VAT calculation would be £247.23 divided by twenty-three, multiplied by three, arriving at £32.24739, or £32.25.

THE SPECIAL RETAILERS SCHEMES

Nine special schemes for retailers are available for choice. Some are suitable only for certain types of business, and some have conditions or limits built into them which mean that not every retailer is allowed to use them. Usually there will be at least one scheme suitable for your particular business.

In some businesses there is only one suitable scheme. In others there may be a choice between three or more schemes. The schemes, which are alphabetically numbered Scheme A, B and so on – J, not I, being the ninth – are fully described in a series of nine booklets issued by the Customs and Excise – HM Customs and Excise Supplements 727A to 727J.

If you are commencing a retail business, or taking one over, you should request these booklets together with the 'Customs and Excise Notice No. 727', a booklet that gives a general explanation of schemes. You may well need expert advice on which of several possible schemes to begin your new business with, or perhaps to which to change over an existing business, because as businesses change or expand it may be advisable to operate a scheme different from the one previously used. You may well also need expert advice on how to operate the scheme once you have selected it.

The best possible advice may be free. It can come from the Customs and Excise Officer at the local main VAT office.

There are, of course, a great number of VAT regulations that are of importance once you are in business but which have no relevance to the questions and problems of acquiring a business, making a choice about the kind of business to acquire, or starting a new business.

There are, however, a number of points that need to be understood by readers proposing to go into business in which they will either have immediate involvement with VAT, or will ultimately have to register if their businesses are successful.

IMPORTS AND EXPORTS
VAT is charged on all imported goods coming into the United Kingdom, except where they are zero-rated, or exempt, or have special relief. Among the goods relieved of VAT if they are imported are samples and exhibition goods; raw materials or other goods imported for a manufacturing process in the UK and then for export; commercial and private vehicles; personal and household effects; equipment on loan or hire; and medical and scientific equipment.

VAT does not apply, however, to services outside the UK given to someone inside the UK.

All exports are zero-rated, and this includes goods exported to the Channel Islands and Eire. But it should be noted that this does not necessarily mean that goods manufactured specifically for export escape tax down the entire chain of production, manufacture and supply. Only the exporter, and in some cases his direct supplier, may give export goods zero rating.

If you are going into business as an exporter you must still register for VAT if and when your 'taxable turnover' reaches the minimum level. And, of course, it may pay you to apply for voluntary registration, anyway, so that you can claim back on Input VAT tax.

AGENTS AND VAT
If you are going into business as an agent, and are therefore supplying goods or services on behalf of other people, you need to ask your local VAT main office for Notice No.710 because there are a number of special considerations.

As an agent you will probably have to handle the invoicing. If the principal for whom you are acting as an agent is not registered for VAT you are allowed to invoice without charging VAT even if you yourself are VAT registered.

On the other hand an agent cannot issue an invoice charging VAT, should he need to do so for a VAT-registered client, if he is not himself VAT registered. As an agent, therefore, voluntary registration should be considered for this reason alone, even if the level of business does not require registration.

CONSTRUCTION BUSINESS

A booklet 'HM Customs and Excise Notice No.708' should be obtained by anyone going into business in the building, construction, maintenance, repair and decoration businesses.

New construction works, improvements and alterations are zero-rated, while repairs, maintenance and decoration are positively-rated. This means that if, as a small jobbing builder, you insulate somebody's roof for them, and it has not previously been insulated, the job is zero-rated. If you do normal roof repairs to the same property, however, the job is then positively-rated.

SECOND-HAND CAR DEALING

Booklet 'HM Customs and Excise Notice No.711' is essential reading for anyone intending to trade in the second-hand car market.

Generally speaking VAT is chargeable on the full sale price of second-hand goods sold by a VAT-registered dealer. For used cars, however, there is a special scheme under which tax is charged only on the dealer's 'margin' – that is the amount by which the selling price exceeds the amount he himself has paid for it.

Although the tax is chargeable only on this profit margin, the 'taxable turnover' for VAT registration purposes must include the total value (exclusive of VAT) of the sale price. There are a number of special considerations connected with this kind of business.

Similar schemes apply to boats and outboard engines, to motor cycles, caravans, electronic organs, antiques, works of art, scientific collections and aircraft. There are booklets available on specific categories of second-hand goods, obtainable from the main local VAT office. These detail whatever special regulations there may be about records and selling certificates.

It is important that anyone trading in any of these special categories of second-hand goods – which are often an area of self-employment that may be developed from home as a part-time occupation – should realize that while the VAT is charged on the profit and not the sale price, liability to register for VAT is based on the whole taxable turnover.

HOTELS, CATERING AND HOLIDAY SERVICES

Special VAT regulations apply to catering, hotels (including guest and boarding houses) and every aspect of holiday services. 'HM Customs and Excise Notice No.709' is the booklet required. These regulations apply to an area of business that attracts many people into self-employment.

Catering, for the purposes of VAT, is taxable as a service. The food and drink served is zero-rated, with certain exceptions like alcoholic drinks, crisps and confectionery which are subject to positive rating anyway.

The take-away food businesses have thrived on the fact that take-away food escapes VAT while the same food, perhaps a sandwich eaten in a café, has a VAT charge added to it. Restaurants and cafés who supply both positive and zero-rated supplies are required to keep two tills unless the local VAT office will agree to the application of an agreed percentage.

Meals supplied in catering establishments to staff, if the ordinary cost of the meal is below £10, escape VAT provided the meals are given free. If the staff makes any payment or have any wage deductions as a consequence, VAT has to be recorded at the full rate. Food and drink consumed by the owner of the business and his family, on the other hand, are subject to the same VAT as that charged to customers.

Hotels, public houses providing lodgings, boarding houses and guest houses – and that of course means taking in paying guests – have to charge VAT at the standard rate. (However, furnished lodgings, bed-sitters and public houses not providing accommodation escape tax.) The tax is paid on the total bill, including any service charge. However, if the stay is of longer duration than four weeks, that part of the bill that relates to accommodation and facilities is subject to VAT reduction, only a percentage of this part of the charge being taxed. Normally this percentage is 20% but this may vary according to the facilities provided.

The section of VAT regulations covered in this particular booklet also covers businesses letting holiday accommodation in houses, flats, house-boats, caravans and letting sites for caravans or tents for 'temporary' stays. All such business is subject to standard rate VAT, but there are special rules for periods of letting above twenty-eight days.

Special regulations apply also to the travel agency business. The travel agent is supplying a service and for this he receives a commission which is normally subject to standard rate VAT.

However, in the case of overseas package holidays, all aspects of what is sold to the holiday maker are either zero-rated (the travel), exempt (the insurance) or outside the scope of UK VAT regulations (the overseas accommodation, etc.). For VAT purposes the travel agent in the case of overseas package holidays is not regarded as selling the holiday on VAT taxable commission, but as himself buying the holiday at a discount equating to the normal commission, and then selling it at full price to the holiday maker. The transaction is zero-rated, and has no VAT imposed upon it.

This chapter has not attempted a comprehensive digest of the operation of Value Added Tax and its regulations, but has merely dealt with those aspects of VAT that may concern people becoming self-employed for the first time.

The structure of the tax is extremely complex, but the reader should not regard involvement as necessarily being a forbidding matter. In any particular business operation only one permutation of the regulations and requirements apply, and once these are familiarized, operating VAT becomes a routine matter.

The local VAT officer is there not to collect tax, but to administer and to give guidance and help. He should be looked upon as an advisor who may help you to recover the VAT you yourself have paid out in connection with your business. Provided you collect enough tax for the Customs and Excise you should get it all back. And in some businesses, by registering, you will get it all back even if you collect no tax at all.

This has been a money-making chapter!

7: *National Insurance*

If you are becoming gainfully self-employed for the first time, whether part-time or full-time, you should at once get in touch with the local Social Security Office, listed in the local telephone directory under the heading 'Health and Social Security, Department of'. Their leaflet NI 41 (National Insurance Guide for the Self-Employed) is concise, essential reading for you and incorporates Form CF 351 (Bank) which authorizes payment by your bank of the National Insurance contributions for which you will be becoming liable, by direct debit – and Form CF 351 (NG) which, as an alternative, authorizes payment of the contributions by automatic debit transfer through the National Giro if you have a Giro account.

Either of these arrangements will save you the bother and nuisance of buying National Insurance stamps from a post office, and sticking them onto a contribution card and then 'cancelling' them each week.

Direct debit arrangements have, of course, safeguards built into them. No direct debit payment is made through an account without the account holder knowing the amount in advance. Direct debit, however, allows the amount to be varied on the advice of the payee – in this case the Department of Health and Social Security, if contribution rates change. If the amount is changed the account holder is advised in advance of the change. The account holder can cancel the arrangement immediately, at any time.

Since, in self-employment, you are almost certainly going

to pay National Insurance contributions, it makes sense to pay in this way, and the system is to be strongly recommended.

In addition to the general leaflet, NI41, there are other leaflets relating to self-employment that are worth mentioning.

Leaflet NI27A (People with Small Earnings from Self-Employment) may be of great importance to you if you are just entering spare-time self-employment because it may help you to avoid paying higher contributions than you need. Exceptions from liability are allowed, but have to be claimed.

Leaflet NI42 (Voluntary Contributions) may be of value in showing you how, if exemptions explained in Leaflet NI27A are taken advantage of, there are alternative voluntary contributions which maintain your entitlements to certain benefits.

Leaflet NP18 (Class 4 National Insurance Contributions) deals with contributions paid by the self-employed on profits or gains within certain higher profit levels.

Leaflet NI48 (Unpaid and Late Paid Contributions) is also worth having in your files for reference.

What you are actually going to pay can best be understood if you appreciate the quite straightforward system of National Insurance.

There are four classes of contributions, three of which provide entitlements the amounts of which depend upon the amount of contributions paid or credited.

The following benefits are the entitlements of contributors to the various classes of contributions :

Class 1
Unemployment benefit
Sickness and invalidity benefits
Maternity benefits
Widows benefits
Retirement pension
Child's special allowance
Death Grant

Class 2
As above, except that there is no unemployment benefit.
Class 3
As in Class 1, except that there is neither unemployment nor sickness and invalidity benefits.
Class 4
No benefits. (The contribution supplements the Class 2 contribution.)

CLASS 1 CONTRIBUTIONS

Class 1 contributions are made by employers on behalf of employees. If your self-employment is part-time and you remain also in work as an employee you will continue to pay Class 1 contributions. If, becoming self-employed, you have formed a limited company then, as an office holder or company director, you are treated as an employee and pay Class 1 contributions.

Class 1 contributions are paid jointly by the employee and the employer, the employer also being responsible for the actual payments and deducting the employee's share of the payment from his wage or salary.

You pay Class 1 contributions in any job in which you earn at least £19.50 a week. Once you qualify to pay the contributions, you do so on *all* earnings in the job, up to a limit of £135 a week.

If you are *not* 'contracted-out' of part of the state pension scheme, you pay 6.5% on *all* your earnings up to £135 a week, and your employer pays 10%. If your employer has a staff pension scheme, you may be 'contracted-out' – which will reduce the graduated pension that supplements the basic State pension. In this case you pay 6.5% of your earnings up to £19.50 a week, but only 4% on earnings between £19.50 and £135 a week. In this case your employer pays 10% up to the lower level of £19.50 and, thereafter, 5.5% up to the upper limit of £135 a week. (All figures given are subject to revision from time to time, but are correct at the time of going to press.)

CLASS 2 CONTRIBUTIONS

Class 2 contributions may be regarded as the contributions paid by the self-employed instead of the Class 1 contributions paid by employees. They are normally paid by all self-employed people between the ages of sixteen and sixty-five in the case of a man or sixty in the case of a woman. The upper age limit exemption applies even if you continue earning, after reaching the age limit.

This insurance does not cover unemployment benefits and it is currently £2.10 a week for everybody. The rates are subject to change from the start of each new tax year in April. Current rates are always published in the latest edition of Leaflet NI 208.

If you cease employment to become self-employed, but have no contribution card for the current year because your earnings as an employee have been below the £19.50 level, you should apply to the local Social Security office for a card (unless you prefer to pay any contributions due from you through a bank or the National Giro).

If you are in employment but you have no contribution card because your earnings are below the minimum level, and you decide to supplement your income by part-time self-employment, you should apply for the card or make arrangements for direct debit payments through a bank or the National Giro.

There are certain circumstances, apart from having reached retirement age, under which you do not have to pay Class 2 contributions in connection with self-employment earnings. These are all related to low levels of income.

You do not have to pay Class 2 contributions as a self-employed person if you are entitled to reduced liability for the current year as a married woman. (Ask for and study Leaflet NI 1.)

Nor do you have to pay if you are entitled to reduced liability as a widow. (Ask for and study Leaflet NI 51.)

And you do not have to pay if, upon application, you are given a certificate of exemption.

Spare-time self-employment deferment or exemption of payment may be obtained in certain circumstances by application.

To avoid exceeding the maximum amount of Class 1 and Class 2 payments payable in any one year, you may apply to defer Class 2 payments until your exact liability has been calculated.

If your earnings in the current tax year are expected to be below a certain level (£1,050 for 1979/80) you may apply for a certificate of exemption. If this is granted you do not require deferment.

If you have a full-time regular job and your earnings from self-employment during the tax year are going to be below the £250 level, then, if you put the case to them, the Department of Health and Social Security may rule that your earnings from self-employment are too small to justify adding Class 2 contributions to the Class 1 contributions you are already paying. In this case you will not need to hold the annually renewable certificate of exemption.

Full-time self-employment exception from liability may be applied for if your total net earnings are below the levels currently in force.

For example, if your earnings were less than £950 during the tax year ending 5 April 1979, and there has been no material change in your circumstances, or if your earnings were expected to be less than £1,050 in the tax year commencing 6 April 1979, you could have applied for exception. (Current figures are published in Leaflet NI 27 A.)

Net earnings are calculated on the basis of the Profit and Loss Account you, or your accountant, need to prepare anyway for Income Tax purposes. Quite simply, the gross earnings have deducted from them the business costs of rent, rates, insurance, printing, stationery, repairs, postage, depreciation allowance and employees' wages.

A cautionary warning must be given about applying for exception when your liability for National Insurance contributions is related only to self-employment earnings.

If you have paid National Insurance Class 1 contributions as an employee in the past, then, if you apply for and are granted exception when you become self-employed, eventually you may cease to be entitled to full National Insurance benefits. If you do not pay contributions over a long period you may lose the advantage of contributions already paid.

Your benefits could be affected in this way.

Retirement Pension You must pay a minimum number or amount of contributions and must have a reasonably complete record of contributions throughout your working life. If you fail to do this you become entitled to only a reduced pension. It is possible to sacrifice your right to any pension at all. If you are married and your wife's pension is based on your contributions, then her rights may be similarly affected. (See Leaflet NI 15 for full information.)

Widow's benefit At risk also would be your wife's right to a full benefit, or to any benefit at all, if you predeceased her (Leaflet NI 13).

Death grant This might not be payable (Leaflet NI 49).

Sickness benefit Entitlement in the year commencing 6 January 1980 will generally depend on the contribution record in the tax year that began on 6 April 1978. (In short current contributions ensure future benefits.) Payment of less than twenty-five Class 2 contributions during the tax year 1978-9 means the sacrifice of the benefit in 1980 (Leaflet NI 16).

Maternity benefit The conditions are similar to those for the sickness benefit.

Invalidity benefit This is normally paid after the sickness benefit has been paid for twenty-eight weeks. It is not payable if there has been no entitlement to the sickness benefit anyway (Leaflet NI 16A). However, it is worth noting that you could still be able to qualify for a non-contributory invalidity pension (Leaflet NI 210 or, for married women, NI 214).

If you wish to apply for exception from liability for Class 2 contributions you should ask for Leaflet NI 27A, which contains the application form CF 10. This two-part form covers both full-time and part-time self-employment situations. If you are given a certificate of exception you may still pay Class 2 contributions voluntarily to preserve your right to the Class 2 benefits.

Share fishermen, as they are known, pay a Special Class 2 contribution entitling them, although they are regarded as self-employed, to unemployment benefits.

A sea-going share fisherman is someone employed in the fishing industry as master or crew member of a British fishing boat manned by more than one person, and who is paid in whole or in part by a share of the profits or gross earnings of the boat.

The special class contribution is £3. A special contribution card is required, and these are issued only by certain Social Security offices, usually ports and fishing centres in England, Scotland and Wales. A special Class 2 stamp is required, and this again is only available at post offices in ports where there is a fishing industry.

A number of special conditions apply to the Share Fishermen scheme, and Leaflet NI47 covers these in detail, and lists the offices from which the special contribution cards may be obtained.

CLASS 3 CONTRIBUTIONS

Voluntary (Class 3) contributions may be paid by people who are not liable to pay Class 1 or Class 2 contributions. These contributions help you to qualify for a limited range of benefits if you have not paid or been credited with enough Class 1 or Class 2 contributions. The most important of the benefits Class 3 contributions help to obtain is the retirement pension. Leaflet NI42 is your required reading and includes the direct debit forms of authority for payment of contributions by a bank or through the National Giro. (Class 3 (flat rate) contributions are currently (1979–80) £2 a week.)

If you are a man over sixty or a woman over fifty-five, and

are therefore nearing pension age, you should ask for advice from the local Social Security office before applying to pay Class 3 contributions.

CLASS 4 CONTRIBUTIONS

An earnings-related contribution to National Insurance on your self-employment profits or gains may be assessed by the Inland Revenue and collected by them. These contributions produce no benefits. Their sole purpose is to ensure that the self-employed as a whole pay a fair share of the cost of pensions and other National Insurance benefits without the lower earning self-employed being penalized by excessively high flat-rate Class 2 contributions.

The self-employed, who qualify for all benefits except unemployment benefit, pay a flat rate of a current £2.10 a week. Unlike the employee, their contribution is not linked to the actual income and increased as it increases. In their case the comparable income is turnover and may be subject to massive deductions (say for purchases of stock or equipment or raw materials). As a matter of equity, when their true profit or gain has been agreed by the Inland Revenue they then become liable for a Class 4 contribution of 5% above £2,250 and up to £7,000 in the tax year. The maximum Class 4 contribution is £237.50. These figures are, of course, liable to annual revision.

Although the contribution is assessed in the same way as tax is assessed, and there are capital allowances and other reliefs, there are no personal allowances and no deductions for private pension or retirement annuity payments – a subject to be discussed in the next chapter of this book.

If a wife has elected for separate tax assessment, or a husband and wife have jointly elected that the wife's income should be taxed as if she were single, then such elections also apply to Class 4 assessments and payments.

In the case of partnerships the Inland Revenue can collect the amount of Class 4 contributions arising from profits or gains made by each partner. If a husband and wife are in partnership, a separate Class 4 contribution is calculated on the wife's share of the profits or gains.

If you are a man over sixty-five or a woman over sixty you are an exception from liability, and in the tax year following the relevant birthday date the Inland Revenue will not make any Class 4 assessment. No application for the exception needs to be made.

If you have more than one job it is always possible for you to pay more than the prescribed amount of contributions in a year. For example, you might be entitled to a refund for the tax year 1978–79 if you paid more than £413.90 in Class 1 and flat-rate Class 2 contributions, or to a refund of Class 4 contributions only if you paid more than £313 in Class 1, Class 2 and Class 4 contributions. Since Class 1 contributions, representing an income as an employee (which could be in the role of a director of your own company) are involved in such a refund situation, it must be pointed out that only the 'employee' part of the Class 1 contribution and not the 'employer' share is counted for this purpose.

You may apply for deferment of payment of Class 4 contributions until such time as it is possible to work out your true liability. This situation arises if you expect to be both employed and self-employed during the current tax year, expect your employee earnings to be substantial, and believe that your *total* contribution liability will exceed the limits given in the preceding paragraph.

If you wish to take this course you require Form CF 359 from the local Inspector of Taxes or the local Social Security office on which to make your application. The completed form should be sent to the Department of Health and Social Security, Class 4 Group, Newcastle Upon Tyne, NE98 1YU. Application should normally be made before 6 April for the tax year commencing on that date, but given acceptable reasons, later application may be allowed.

If deferment is agreed then the calculation and collection of your Class 4 contributions will be transferred from the Inland Revenue to the Department of Health and Social Security who will be supplied, by the Inland Revenue, with a certificate showing what they have agreed your profits or gains to be up to the limit of £7,000.

Certain people, such as actors or musicians, may pay Class 1 contributions on earnings as employees. Because they are assessed under Schedule D they may face liability for Class 4 contributions. In such circumstances the amount of Class 4 contributions will be reduced, provided deferment of liability is applied for and obtained.

Share fishermen may also be liable for Class 4 contributions. Since they may have their Income Tax deducted at source under the PAYE scheme, in their case the Class 4 contribution is also deducted at source unless application is made for deferment. Deferment could be justified if the share fisherman role is part-time and there is also payment of Class 1 contributions in connection with part-time shore work as an employee.

SELF-EMPLOYMENT AFTER PENSIONABLE RETIREMENT AGE

For many people self-employment begins with reaching retirement age and leaving full-time employment. It may be embarked upon against a background of one or more of the following separate sources of unearned income:

1. There may be an income from interest or dividends from the invested savings of a lifetime, probably taxed at source.
2. There may be a company pension which, if there is liability for income tax, will be taxed under the PAYE coding system at source just like the salary it has replaced.
3. There will be a retirement pension from the Department of Health and Social Security which, in the case of a man, may incorporate a dependency increase for his wife even if she is below her retirement age of sixty, so long as she can be considered as retired.

The State retirement pension is a part of the total income for tax purposes. If there is a company pension, deductions from it will be made by the coding system to cover the liability on the State pension. The State pension is, however, a conditional source of income for the first five years. An Earnings Rule may penalize you if your skills and energies prove to be too remunerative during these years. The pension may be reduced or may be sacrificed altogether.

A retirement pensioner (up to the age of seventy for a man or sixty-five for a woman) is now allowed to earn up to £52 net a week and still receive the full State pension. This ceiling figure allows deductions to be made first from gross earnings for a list of 'allowable expenses' which includes travel, tools and equipment, cost of premises, protective clothing if used, subscriptions, care of dependents, and an allowance for working hours meals. The listed deductions are given specifically by the Department for the guidance of the pensioner whose earnings are of a casual and occasional nature. In any week in which the earnings after deductions are £52 or more the pensioner must notify the Department of Health and Social Security.

On earnings between £52 and £56 a week, for every 10p earned 5p is deducted from the State pension. Above £56 a week, for every 5p earned 5p is deducted from the State pension until the pension becomes extinguished.

For the self-employed – the people engaged in business on their own account on a regular basis – the earnings are accepted as the profits agreed by the Inland Revenue for Income Tax purposes. Since these cannot be forecast, and are only agreed annually after the end of a fiscal year, the usual procedure is that the pension is 'suspended' until the profit figure agreed by the Inland Revenue is eventually known. Interim payments, equivalent to the pension, are made instead of the pension. If when the profit figure is agreed with the Inland Revenue, it is below the earnings rule level currently at £52 a week, the interim payments are regarded as having been paid as the retirement pension. If the figure exceeds the £52 a week for the tax year, then any over-payment must be paid back to the Department of Health and Social Security.

If your self-employment income becomes high, or is 'spasmodic' and may include occasional large sums which could suddenly be paid at the end of a tax year, you have to be prepared for the fact that you may have to repay the whole of a year's pension.

For those entering self-employment after reaching retirement age, after a normal working life in which both income tax and national insurance contributions have always been deducted from their wages or salary, one of the major problems may be the budgeting necessary to fund both for future income tax payments and for possible Social Security pension repayments.

The best way of handling this situation is to apply for payment of the pension (or interim payment made in lieu of it) to be paid quarterly in arrears. This money may then be funded if self-employment is providing an at least comparable income. In such a case it is wise not to regard it as freed capital until the tax year's profits have been agreed and the right to the pension, or the need to pay back some or all of it, is established.

There is an important point to be remembered in this connection. If there is a good company pension it is possible that up to about £600 of tax may have been deducted from it on account of State pension interim payments made to a married man with a dependent wife under the age of sixty. If repayment of either the whole or of any part of the interim payments has to be made, and PAYE tax has already been paid out of a company pension, then a certificate of the repayment must be obtained from the Department of Health and Social Security and used to claim the appropriate refund of tax from the Inland Revenue.

8: Self-employment pensions and insurance

Possibly one of the most important services this book may give to its readers is to examine what are generally known as 'personal pensions'. Personal pensions represent the biggest tax-exemption benefit available to the self-employed and the 1980 Finance Act improved these benefits dramatically. Yet under twenty per cent of the self-employed use their advantage.

Since 1975, the self-employed have been paying into the National Insurance system, by their Class 4 contributions, described in the previous chapter, an earnings-related levy. Yet the new State earnings-related pension scheme leaves the self-employed out in the cold. The only extra pension benefit they can take is the one which only one in five of them does take – letting the government pay at least 30% of their premiums into a private pension fund which itself escapes Corporation taxation and the penalties of capital gains. It is foolish to let such a bargain go begging.

THE CHOICE BETWEEN ENDOWMENT AND 'PENSION' POLICIES

The self-employed have to recognize that, for them, a State earnings-related pension is not yet even on the horizon. All they can anticipate getting by way of a pension, if and when they want to retire, or can afford to, will be the basic 'Old Age Pension'. The label is derogatory and the amount is derisory.

The need to make independent arrangements for an

adequate income for retirement should be of concern from the very day that self-employment begins, and this is why. According to insurance actuaries, if you retire at sixty you have an average seventeen and a half more years of life ahead of you if you are a man, or twenty more years if you are a woman. It could be a good deal more, and the average life expectancy is going up all the time.

This means that probably more than a quarter of your whole life since birth and a third of your life as an adult is likely to lie ahead of you if you retire at what is expected to become the average retirement age in the near future. If you can see future retirement in this perspective, then the need to make provision for what will be a considerable part of your life will assume the importance it should be given.

Since the government will not contribute to any form of capital saving you make, but will tax the interest on such savings, the sensible thing is to put the savings into a fund to which the government *will* contribute – a pension insurance policy.

You have two main choices. You may take out an endowment policy, or you can choose a personal pension policy. First consider the endowment policy.

Endowment policy A with-profits endowment policy matures at the age at which you anticipate retiring. When it matures you take the capital sum and with it, if you want a pension, you buy an annuity.

You do not have to take out the annuity with the same insurance company with which you took out the endowment policy. It could well be that at the time your policy matures other better annuity rates are available from other companies. The rates can vary by as much as 20%.

An endowment policy has an increasing surrender value all the time you are paying your premiums. If at any time you need a business loan, here is the very security your bank manager will find acceptable and it can be temporarily assigned to cover an overdraft or other loan arrangement.

Normally, your premium payments are allowed tax relief

at 15% (from 6 April 1981) but there are restrictions: you will get relief on all premiums you pay up to one-sixth of your income or £1,500, whichever is the greater.

With pensions resulting from an endowment policy, only part of the annuity is taxable, as investment income.

Personal pensions With a personal pension you cannot take out the entire capital sum for use or reinvestment as you see fit. Indeed, until very recently, the reinvestment into an income-paying annuity was automatically with the same insurance company at their current rate, regardless of the fact that other companies might be offering much higher rates.

You are only allowed to take out in cash a tax-free sum equal to three times the amount of pension remaining after the deduction if the most favourable way of having the pension paid is selected.

You cannot use a personal pension as security for a loan if your business runs into financial difficulties, as you can with an endowment insurance policy. On the other hand the pension cannot usually be touched by creditors.

There are limits to the percentage of your income you can invest in a personal pension. There are improved age-linked limits to the total amount you may invest in a year for those born prior to 1915.

With pensions arising from a personal pension policy the entire pension is subject to normal 'earned income' taxation.

A comparison between the two choices based on these facts would suggest that the endowment policy has all the advantages, especially if a close inspection of the figures by your professional insurance advisor shows, as it would at the present time, that if £500 a year of income were put into each of the two types of policies, the endowment policy could produce the higher pension.

However this is not the way to consider the matter. The **true** comparison has to be based on the fact that £335 invested in a personal pension *will* produce a much better pension than

£412.50 invested in an endowment policy.

With tax relief at 15%, the £500 invested in an endowment policy actually costs the policy holder £425. But in the case of a personal pension, since *full* relief is given at the taxpayer's highest tax rate, the £500 policy costs the policy holder only £350, the government paying the rest if the relevant earnings are below a £11,250 a year limit. Above £11,250 the tax is at the rate of 40%. From £13,250 to £16,750 it is at 45%. From £16,750 to £22,250 it is at 50%. From £22,250 to £22,750 it is at 55%. And – future millionaires should note – over £22,750 it is at 60%. Before the 1980 Finance Act the upper rate was 83%!

Thus, under personal pension policies – of which there are four main types to consider – these are by far the better choice in most circumstances.

The final choice, however, must always be based on factors that actuaries cannot take into account. You may want the reassuring feeling that you could raise money on your policy at some future date in the furtherance of long-term ambitions you are not telling anybody about yet. You may prefer the endowment policy for the same 'surrender value' reasons because secretly you lack the self-assurance needed to commit yourself to locking up a part of your income in a way that means you can never really get to it as capital again.

And after all, that is what self-employment is all about – the right to make independent decisions.

GETTING PROFESSIONAL ADVICE

Whatever options of personal choice you exercise, only professional advice, related to your individual case and needs, can give you the full range of choices recommendable to you.

Your accountant, solicitor or bank manager could, any one of them, give you useful and sound advice. It is recommendable, however, that in a specialized matter as complex as insurance, and as important as are the investments for eventual retirement, you should consult an insurance broking company.

Yellow Pages directories list brokers under this heading,

but it is sensible to deal with a company which has experts to handle the various aspects of insurance that may apply to you and your particular business, rather than one which may specialize in a particular aspect of insurance.

For the convenience of readers who have no advisors to introduce them, one company which covers every type of insurance is Wigham Poland Ltd, Bevington House, 24/26 Minories, London EC3N 1BY (Tel: 01-481 0505).

Where the enquiry is going to cover more than one aspect of insurance, contact is made first, by letter or telephone, with the director of one specific category of insurance, subsequently allowing him to channel other enquiries to the expert advisors of the other categories.

The value of a broker is not only the depth and width of his experience, but the objectivity of his recommendations.

RELEVANT EARNINGS AND MAXIMUM ANNUAL PENSION INVESTMENT

The following table shows the percentage of the relevant income that may be invested annually in a personal pension. The 1980 Finance Act increased the percentages by an all-round $2\frac{1}{2}\%$ and swept away the imposition of a ceiling on contributions.

Date of birth	% of relevant earnings
1907 or before	30
1908-09	27
1910-11	24
1912-13	21
1914-15	18
1916 onwards	15

The considerably increased percentages have been allowed to older people because they face the disadvantage of late entry into such insurance when it was first introduced in 1956. Such concessions were devised to take into account such facts as, for instance, someone becoming self-employed at the age of thirty-five and investing £500 gross in a personal pension, who could expect to have a fund of about £83,500 at the age of sixty-five, while the same annual investment by someone becoming self-employed at fifty-five would only have a fund of about £8,650 available to provide a tax-free cash sum and to buy an annuity.

These age-linked increases of the limits do not apply to people already receiving, or entitled in the future, to a pension from previous employment.

Net relevant earnings in this context mean the gross earned income (with certain deductions).

Personal pension schemes are also allowed to include life insurance, payable to the Estate, the premiums for this part of the cover still gaining full tax relief at the highest level of tax being paid, instead of relief at 15% only, as in the case of ordinary life insurance. As the 1980 edition of this book is being updated, the subject of personal pension schemes for full-time self-employed who have carried-forward pension benefit from earlier employment is one of those grey areas of interpretation which justify the recommendation that professional advice must always be sought in these matters.

Life insurance contributions taken out on these especially favourable terms in conjunction with a personal pension policy are limited to contributions not greater than 5% of the relevant earnings and are subject to a maximum of £1,000. The life insurance inclusion is not additional to the pension policy concessions, but represents an alternative way of using part of the tax concessions, the total maximum limits remaining the same.

The pension can be begun to be drawn at any chosen time between the ages of sixty and seventy-five, and drawing it does not depend on actual retirement. In occupations where retirement is before the age of sixty – for example pilots and women nurses at fifty-five, and sportsmen, like footballers, at fifty – the pension may be drawn at the earlier retirement date.

There are other exceptions, making allowances for every kind of job and every kind of circumstance. The 'net relevant earnings' rules, for instance, are varied for professional people like doctors. And in case of enforced early retirement for health reasons, the pension may be taken early.

TYPES OF PENSION SCHEMES

One effect of the inflationary spiral that has become a fact of life is that investment limits, rates, percentages, maximums and regulations are constantly changing. As they change the business world alters, modifies and revises its own schemes and offers.

The new 'shopping option', introduced while this book was in preparation, which allows the holder of a personal pension policy to transfer the value of his policy at retirement age to a different insurance company offering more favourable annuity rates, creates a whole new improved situation.

In choosing one of the very many alternative personal pension policies available, it used to be necessary, at the time of taking out the policy, to consider both the ultimate value of the pension fund being accumulated and also the annuity arrangements offered by the same policy.

Now the decision needs only to be made in connection with the possible future value of the pension fund, and how it is going to be created. The rates, terms and type of annuity become matters in which decisions may be deferred until actual retirement.

There are many variations available among four basic types of personal pension schemes.

Non-profit This type of policy gives the highest *guaranteed* sum, but under inflationary circumstances it is unlikely to match other policies in the long term. If self-employment is taken up when only a few years are left before planned retirement, then this kind of policy should be considered. If you are under fifty-five it is not for you.

With profits In this kind of policy a bonus is added on an annual basis. There is a guaranteed benefit, but the bonuses, once they have been declared, are irrevocable and

begin contributing to an increase of the ultimate benefit.
Deposit administration This kind of policy works exactly as its categorization suggests. It is a financial administration of a deposit account, in the same sense of that term as a bank refers to an investment, or deposit account.

The insurance company deducts a 'management' charge from each premium, and the balance goes into the member's account to earn interest at currently prevailing rates. Some insurance companies offer a guarantee that this interest will never fall below that being offered at the time by building societies.

This kind of policy is, of course, simple investment to produce a fund at retirement age partly available in cash, and partly convertible into an annuity on the best terms available at the time.

The advantage against investing the same money oneself possibly into share accounts in building societies is that, in effect, at least one-third of the investment premiums are paid by the State.

Unit linked The unit linked schemes are inevitably speculative. In very simple layman terms they mean that the premiums paid represent contributions into a fund used for professional market investment. There can be, therefore, a speculative element about them. The minimum pension may, in some fully linked schemes, be much lower than those guaranteed by other schemes. At the same time the unit linked scheme is the only real opportunity there is, in the field of pension insurance, of keeping the level of inflation and the level of ultimate pension in step.

ANNUAL PENSION DECISIONS

With so many considerations, and an infinite number of different policies offering many variations of detail, and with constantly changing financial situations, it is fortunate that the self-employed do not have to commit themselves once and for all to any one particular type of policy to qualify for the tax benefits.

Tax relief applies equally to regular and single payment premiums. This means that you may spread the risk between different types of policies and different companies. It means that you can invest different amounts in different years, in different policies, depending upon the way your business has gone in the particular years.

If you commit yourself to regular premiums, in a bad year the premium might be more than the $17\frac{1}{2}\%$ of your relevant earnings, and you may therefore lose some of your tax relief in the very year when you most needed it.

COMPANY SCHEMES

Very special consideration has to be given by people who, although eligible for personal pension insurance schemes, also have the opportunity to join company operated pension schemes.

Specifically this situation relates to self-employed people who set up, or acquire ready-made, limited liability companies, and who become directors of their own companies. For them there are no limits on relevant earnings or maximum contributions just before retiring if they join a pension scheme operated for the company employees.

In schemes of this kind the 'company' makes its contributions and there are no upper limits on these. The regulations and conditions in such cases are very complex and any self-employed director of his own company will, anyway, have an expert professional insurance broker to guide him along his most advantageous individual path.

In a series of 'Practical Pensions' articles, *The Sunday Times Business News*, beginning in January 1978, published an examination of fourteen different cases from the books of Wigham Poland which dealt in detail with some of the considerations in such cases.

Here the only advice that can be offered to the reader is that if a company situation exists in your self-employment, it must pay you to consult a professional financial advisor about the 'pension investment' advantages inherent in your situation.

CHOICE OF PENSION PAYMENT SCHEMES

This book is concerned with becoming self-employed, not with having been self-employed. Nevertheless, in the necessarily important discussion about making provisions for retirement as soon as one becomes self-employed, and when the terms are most favourable, it is relevant to consider briefly what one is buying and what the later options will be.

It is not permitted to convert a personal pension policy into hard cash in the way that an endowment policy can be converted. Instead, as already mentioned, a tax-free percentage, equalling three times the remaining pension taken on the 'most favourable terms', is allowed. This option should be exercised even if the capital sum is not required for, say, a retirement holiday cruise. The tax-free commuted part of the pension can be invested in, say building society paid-up shares which represent readily available capital if it should ever be required. In full or in part it can be moved into tax-exempt, index-linked retirement National Savings certificates. It can be put into speculative Premium Bonds. Unlike the money committed to an annuity, it is capital that may be moved about.

The part of the fund that has to be transferred into an annuity can be paid out to the policy holder as a pension in several different ways :

1. He may choose to have a pension that is the same in each successive year.
2. He may choose to have one that increases each year by a predetermined compound rate, to keep in pace with current inflationary trends at the time of retirement.
3. He may choose to have a pension that varies from year to year in relationship to investment fund returns.
4. He may put aside part of his pension to become a personal pension for his wife in the event that he predeceases her, the

limitation being that her pension, so secured, must not be greater than the reduced pension he retains.

5. He can arrange for a pension annuity, guaranteeing the pension over a limited number of years, the maximum being ten years.

GENERAL CONSIDERATIONS

Making full use of the tax concessions offered self-employed people – and also to employees where there is no firm's pension scheme related to their employment – has other advantages besides that of the tax relief on premiums.

The insurance company's 'pension fund' into which these contributions are paid, is itself – unlike other similar funds – exempt from tax. It pays no income tax on its own investments. It pays no capital gains. It can accumulate funds for the policy holder, in a kind of 'wonderland' in which the Inland Revenue does not even exist in a bad dream!

Because the regulations allow flexibility, many schemes allow the policy holder to vary the amount of premiums from year to year, according to the fluctuating profitability of their businesses.

BUSINESS INSURANCE

This chapter has so far concerned itself solely with the branch of insurance that deals with pensions. Personally important though this subject is, it is the tip of the iceberg. Insurance of many different kinds becomes an imposed responsibility on most of the self-employed. This is why it makes good sense to use the services of a broker.

There are about three hundred insurance companies in the UK, many of which specialize in particular aspects of insurance. Insurance bought through a broker – who will advise you exactly what insurance you need, negotiate it for you, collect your premiums, and help you if you have to make a claim – does not cost you more. The broker is paid by the insurance company.

Apart from commercial vehicle insurance, where the

important point to note is that private car insurance can be extended to cover trade purposes by arrangement with the insurers, most business risk can be covered by 'package policies'.

This is a good deal cheaper in many cases than taking out separate policies for different types of risk. It could however be unsatisfactory. You could be paying for some kinds of insurance you don't need, and not getting enough cover for your real risks.

It is sensible anyway to look at the various kinds of business risks and to decide which of them you may need to cover. The broker will then recommend how to arrange the right balance of insurance in your particular case.

EMPLOYEE ACCIDENTS

If your business is one in which you employ other people and one of your employees has an accident at work, the employee is entitled to the industrial injuries benefits provided for by the combined contributions made by him or her and yourself to National Insurance. Nevertheless, if the accident arose through your negligence, that of another employee, or was caused by a faulty machine, the injured employee might be able to sue you for damages. Since 1972 employers have been required by law to take out an Employers Liability Insurance policy, which gives cover of at least £2 million. This insurance is not compulsory in the case of domestic servants, independent contractors and certain close relatives – although it is wise to extend the policy to cover claims from them. The cost of these policies is usually related to the size of the wages or salary bill, and differs according to both the general business risks, and those of the particular employee.

PUBLIC LIABILITY INSURANCE

This is an equally essential type of insurance, especially to traders. It has to cover every kind of mishap from the shop customer tripping over a faulty step or floorboard, to an outbreak of food poisoning traced back to goods sold at one particular shop, or a fire disaster in which there might be loss of life.

Insurance companies usually limit their liability in connection with any one accident, usually to between £25,000 and £250,000. These days it is wise to be covered for at least £100,000 for any one accident.

The small print in these policies needs careful vetting. You *must* be covered for the consequences of a fire. You *must* be covered for any accident or illness, or any damage or loss arising from products you sell, use or manufacture.

Most such policies exclude damage caused in connection with vehicles, lifts, aircraft, or faulty design of goods. Special policies are needed in connection with risks of this kind when the dangers are inherent in the business. The cover should also extend to apply to imported products and goods and the claims that could arise in connection with them. Ensure that you can claim for costs and legal expenses you might have to bear before settlement of a claim. Cases can be protracted!

FIRE POLICIES

These normally also cover lightning and gas explosions and can be extended to cover other hazards. You should consider whether or not your policy should include these extras and, if so, which you need.

Flood and storm damage may require cover, especially if in your business you have equipment or stock vulnerable to weather damage, or if you have business premises which are in areas where there is a flood risk.

Burst pipes and tanks are an inexpensively covered risk, but one worth taking cover out against because such damage *may* come from other, adjoining premises.

Subsidence is a risk which has been traditionally linked with the almost non-existent UK risk of earthquakes. The prolonged drought of a year or so ago demonstrated, however, that it is a risk for which business premises should carry the very cheaply acquired cover.

Explosions A standard fire policy covers explosions but only in a limited way when they are caused by gas used to heat the building. A wider risk may in some cases, be worth covering.

Aircraft This is a remote risk but it does increase with property situated close to airports.

Impact This kind of cover is related to vehicles running off the road and, in rural areas, to damage caused by horses and cattle. Claims are usually excluded if the insured or his employee or relative was in charge of whatever caused the impact.

Malicious damage If you have a shop in an area subject to vandalism, or close to a football ground, this has become an almost essential 'extension clause' to a fire policy.

SHOP WINDOWS AND PLATE GLASS

This is a specialist type of insurance, and many specialist insurers have a 24-hour glass replacement service, having their own glaziers, delivery vans and stocks of glass. The policy is worth having just for this service alone. It covers windows, doors, showcases, mirrors, and usually provides for the cost of temporary boarding up if this is necessary. It should also cover damage by falling or broken glass, and any losses caused by a disturbance of normal trading conditions.

THEFT

One of the most important of business insurance policies and commercial policies covers damage, as well as actual losses by theft, when the thief has entered business premises using force. Trading stock, equipment, fittings and fixtures are normally all covered, but both the premium and the details of the cover will vary according to the risk being covered. An insurance representative may visit the premises and advise generally on security measures and even impose conditions before giving cover.

Premiums may be reduced if approved types of locks, and alarm systems are fitted.

MONEY
The cost of this kind of insurance also depends on security arrangements and the amount of cover required. In the context of the policy, money also means cheques, postal orders, stamps and National Insurance stamps. These policies can cover money in transit to and from the bank. They may cover business money taken home, but there is usually a fairly low-level limit on money left overnight in business premises.

PROFITS
This is a policy which gives cover for the interruption to business that might follow as a consequence of any of the risks covered in the fire policy and its associated hazards.

The loss of profits policy has to cover you for continuing rents, rates, mortgages, special advertising, salaries to employees and the subsequent use of temporary premises if your business is interrupted. You should include any liability you might have to employees under the Contracts of Employment and Redundancy Payment Act. In certain cases you should extend the policy to cover fire or flood at the premises of a supplier upon whom you rely.

It is wise to insure for a sum that would cover your estimated loss if your business came to a halt for a whole year. By arrangement provision may be made with the insurer for a very considerable rebate if your gross profits for the year of the cover actually fell very much behind your estimate. This is the kind of negotiation a broker can best handle for you.

FRAUD
A fidelity guarantee policy may be important to you if you buy or start a business in which you have the role of employer, and you are vulnerable to any dishonesty among your employees. You may take a policy that covers all employees, or one that covers only those who are in a position to cause you losses. The insurers will investigate any specified employees.

This is a policy designed to cover substantial losses. It could apply in businesses where the goods have high value, like jewellery businesses. It could apply in businesses where large sums of money are handled.

GOODS IN TRANSIT
In businesses where goods or produce have to be delivered to the purchasers, a goods in transit policy will provide insurance cover from the time of loading to the time of unloading. The same cover can be applied to goods sent by post. Insurance can be arranged for single or for regular deliveries. This kind of insurance is of especial value where fragile or breakable goods have to be delivered.

SPECIAL BUSINESSES INSURANCES
All the classes of insurance that have been briefly outlined so far can be applied to a wide range of businesses. There are a number of other generally recognized policies which usually relate to particular businesses.

These cover the special indemnity needed by *garage owners* relating to stored cars, claims resulting from negligent repair work, and to risks related to petrol pumps.

Hotel proprietors policies are usually 'general business policies' with extended cover given to cover special liability to guests and their luggage.

Farmers have two categories of special policies. One covers cattle and horses, and the other covers claims arising from crop spraying, milk contamination, infected meat or produce of any kind.

There are also specific policies which deal with lifts, and others that cover industrial plant of different kinds. And there is a 'professional indemnity' policy, versions of which apply to most professions. Many professional associations do, in fact, make special arrangements for their members. Authors may take out such policies to protect themselves against libel claims, or claims arising from errors.

Licensed premises policies are catered for by a licensing insurance, which covers restaurants, public houses, theatres, cinemas and all other businesses where a continuation of the licence is essential to business. The policy compensates if circumstances arise in which a renewal of a licence is refused. It covers the cost of appeals and of loss of business until the licence is renewed.

The question of licences is a broad one, and is dealt with in the next chapter.

9:Licences

No licence is needed to become self-employed. No permission is required. In this country anyone who wishes to do so may set up in business and become his or her own boss. And if that statement sounds familiar, you read it on the first page of the first chapter of this book.

Having reached this chapter it will come as no surprise to find the qualification that, nevertheless, few people will get far in self-employment without coming up against a need to be licensed.

THE SCOPE OF LICENSING
Consider one or two examples.

If you have taken over a small general shop and subsequently, in the period before 5 November, wish to sell fireworks, you will find that you need a licence. This one is issued by the Customs and Excise.

If you take over a household goods shop you will find that you need a licence, in your own name, to sell any of a whole range of taken for granted goods, including methylated spirits, drain cleaners, caustic soda and spirits of salts. The licensing authority is the Trading Standards Department of the County Council.

Probably nobody comes off worse than the publican. The broad outline of the regulations covering the sale of alcohol – in restaurants, hotels and public houses, on boats and at off-licences – are statutory. However, wide variations of detail may apply in different areas and in different magistrates' courts. The application form is obtained from the Clerk to the local Magistrates' Court. When completed it is submitted back to him with a copy to the police.

The procedures can be vexatious to the publican. If, for example, one of his regulars is getting married and wants a reception that will extend outside normal permitted trading hours, the publican needs to know a month ahead so that he may make the necessary special application. He must have a formal, written request from the bride and groom giving details of the date, time and place of the wedding. The police will make routine enquiries to confirm to the magistrate that these details are correct. The publican may have to attend the court and may have to wait through a whole list of minor criminal cases before his application is given a 'rubber stamp' approval.

Fortunately most licensing procedures are, in a sense, no more than the formal registrations that are recognizably in the general interest. And being specific, the individual is rarely concerned with more than one of those that relate to his or her particular trade.

The principal licensing and registration functions of local authorities outside Greater London cover such subjects as: animal establishments; betting and lotteries; amusements with prizes; betting tracks; pools promoters; small lotteries; calcium carbide storage; canal boats; caravan sites; cinematograph exhibitions; common lodging houses; dairies; explosives; food – premises and vehicles used in connection with the manufacture and sale of certain foods (specifically ice cream, sausages and preserved foods); game dealers; Hackney carriages; horses, ponies and donkeys standing for hire: the licensing of proprietors and drivers; knackers yards; late night refreshment houses; moneylenders; music and dancing; nurseries and child minders; nurses' agencies; nursing homes; old persons homes; old metal and marine store dealers; pawnbrokers; pedlars; performing animals; pet shops; petroleum storage; pleasure boats, proprietors and boatmen; poisons –

registrations of persons other than 'authorized sellers'; porters; premises where rag flock materials are used; refreshment houses; riding establishments; slaughterhouses; slaughtermen; servants' registries; theatres; theatrical employers; waste food boiling plants.

It is also a matter for registration with the local authority if a Jewish shopkeeper wishes to substitute Sunday trading until 2 pm in place of Saturday trading.

Where this kind of registration or licensing is required (including the licensing and the registration of vehicles for renting or plying for hire, or of boats where a licensing authority may be linked with a particular river, canal or waterway), no particular problems exist. These are matters in which the vendor of a business being sold, or the business transfer agency arranging the sale, will explain the requirements. They are matters with which the solicitor acting for the purchaser will deal automatically, as a matter of routine, just as he deals with apportionments of rates. In a sense they are simply the regulations of business.

There are two areas of licensing that require deeper examination, however – planning permission and consumer credit licensing.

CHANGE OF USAGE

Every business must be conducted at or from premises of some kind. This is as true of the home typist's dining-room as it is of the freelance photographer's dark room, the doctor's surgery, the corner shop, office accommodation in a city skyscraper, the farm and the industrial factory. The law dealing with the use of all property – specifically section 53 of the Town and Country Planning Act, 1971 – is therefore of importance to anybody becoming self-employed.

If you are acquiring a ready-made business, then the particular business use of the premises will have already been established by the vendor, and it will be part of your solicitor's function to check that this is so.

If you are starting a new business, of any kind, one of the

first questions you must ask yourself is whether there is any reason why you should not use, or might not be allowed to use, the premises, where or from which you propose to conduct your business, for the purpose you intend.

The answer will usually need common sense rather than an understanding of the Town and Country Planning Act.

If, for example, you are going to work part-time from home, using one end of the living-room for a quiet, non-mechanical job like designing greeting cards, it is safe to assume that you do not need consent for a change of usage from 'residential' to 'light industrial'. Your property will remain basically residential and there will be no element of nuisance to your neighbours, nor any aspect of your business detrimental to their interests. Indeed, unless you tell them nobody will ever know about your part-time work.

But if you are already living in a private house on the main street of a small town, you cannot simply turn your front room into a shop, taking down the curtains, filling the window with a display of goods for sale and leaving your front door open for customers to enter. In this case you would be making a positive change in the use of the property, and you would need to have consent. Quite apart from the views of the Planning Committee of the local authority, such consent could not be given without your neighbours first having been given an opportunity to object. Very possibly, too, an examination of the deeds of your property would reveal that at the time of building a covenant was entered into prohibiting business use of the premises. In default of objections, such covenants may be legally set aside if their original intentions no longer apply, but this can be a lengthy matter.

Since most freehold property is subject to restrictive covenants, anybody proposing to work from home would be well advised to look at their deeds.

If the premises from which you propose to conduct your new business have been, say, previously a shop selling antiques, you cannot take them and open a restaurant in them. That, too, is a change of usage.

If the premises from which you propose to operate *have* been used as a restaurant but you propose to use them for light industrial manufacturing, then you will not only need consent for a change of use of the property but, if the area is not zoned for light industry, you would be wasting your time even making an application.

If the premises *have* been used for light industrial work but you propose to put in heavy machinery and use them for heavy industrial manufacturing, the same rule will apply. Not only will you need consent, but if the area is not zoned for heavy industrial work you would be wasting your time in making the application.

PLANNING PERMISSION

Whether you are launching a new business or acquiring an existing one, sooner or later it is likely that you will require planning permission. It may well be that you make your purchase of a business, or of the separate purchase of a property freehold or leasehold, one that is 'subject to planning permission'.

Assuming that you may use the premises for your proposed purpose, or can obtain permission for any change of use that may be involved, under the Town and Country Planning Act consent is still necessary for most structural alterations to existing buildings or for extensions.

Thus, if you are working only part-time from home but want to build a workshop in the garden, or make an extension to your home to provide an office, you must first have planning permission. In the same way, if you want to change the frontage of a shop, or put in the toilets that may be necessary if you are opening a restaurant, or if you need to erect a completely new industrial manufacturing building, you must have planning permission.

Planning permission is obtained from the local authority and may be granted in two stages.

Initially you may make an application only for 'outline planning permission'. The purpose of this is to establish that, in principle, you will be allowed to do what you propose. It allows you to count on the final permission being granted, and to go ahead with your arrangements, before you are ready to submit the detailed drawings and architect's plans. A full planning application is then made later.

If your project does involve building, then the expert you now need is an architect. Architects are listed in the *Yellow Pages* directories, but the person you need if you propose to give a face-lift to a village high street shop is not the architect you would want if you had a Centre Point or a South Bank National Theatre type of project in mind.

Getting the right architect could be very important to you. Professional proficiency may be taken for granted. The problem often is that it is not the architect's imagination that is wanted, but yours; that he or she has to see into your mind, see the vague picture there and give its reality sharpness of detail. This is one area in which this book can offer the reader little practical advice. In most cases, however, any competent professional architect will do and will handle the whole matter for you.

If you have only minor problems and propose simply to instruct a builder or carpenter, or even do the work yourself, then you should contact the Borough Surveyor's office at the local authority offices and arrange an appointment. Your applications will be made on Form TP1, (Parts 1 and 2) and these are obtained from his office. The 'Notes to Applicants' issued with Form TP1, make the comment: 'It may be helpful to you to call at the District Council offices to discuss your proposals before you complete the application'.

Never refuse an offer of help from an expert, especially if it is given free. The invitation is well worth taking up, but when you go to the meeting there is one matter upon which you should be ready to give information – your own rights in connection with the property.

Under the Town and Country Planning Act, the local authority cannot entertain any application for planning permission that is not accompanied by one or other of four certificates. The certificates are on the forms you will be given. You need to know which one is applicable in your own case.

Certificate A: This certifies that you are the freeholder or have a lease with at least seven years unexpired of all the land.

Certificate B: If certificate A does not apply, certificate B certifies that you have given notice to the owner (that is to the freeholder, or to a leaseholder who has at least ten years lease remaining).

Certificates C and D: These are both used if you have made efforts to trace other owners and have failed.

All these certificates require documentary evidence in support of them.

If you make structural alterations to a property or build any extension without obtaining planning permission you should have had, then an enforcement order to restore the property to its former state might well be issued. The possibility that planning permission would probably have been granted if it had been applied for may not always count. Local authorities tend to test their muscle with offenders.

And if you make a change in the use of a property without seeking consent, the local authority can get tough about this too. They have the power to issue a 'stop' order, bringing your business to an abrupt halt. If this is not obeyed within four days there is a liability to a fine.

Make friends with the people at the Town Hall.

CONSUMER CREDIT LICENCES

Many of the laws that until recently have governed the giving of credit to customers, hire-purchase, and the leasing or hiring of goods or equipment, dated back to the last century. The consequence was that sometimes the customer lacked legal protection against unscrupulous traders, and that what the credit was really costing was often concealed by the way in which it was explained to the buyer.

The Consumer Credit Act, 1974, was designed to sweep away all the earlier and out-of-date legislation and replace it with a set of simple rules that would apply to all kinds of credit business and would give proper protection to both consumer and trader. Even more important the intention of the Act was to ensure that only fair-dealing traders could give credit and charge interest.

This 'new deal' has created the biggest licensing system ever set up, apart from the short-term emergency measures taken in times of war.

It was calculated that at least 100,000 licences would have to be issued. The introduction of the system has been gradual, the first categories of licences becoming required from 1 October 1977. At the moment many small traders escape the net by a 'deferment' limit, which allows them to 'give tick' or 'put it on the slate' on a small scale.

The licences are issued by the Director General of Fair Trading. If you think that a business you are starting, or are acquiring, requires a licence, you should write for an application form, or for information and advice, to the Office of Fair Trading, Bromyard Avenue, Acton, London W3 7BB (Tel: 01-749 9151). You can also obtain application forms and explanatory literature from the Trading Standards Department of your local authority. This department is sometimes known and listed as the Consumer Protection Department or the Weights and Measures Department.

In Northern Ireland the Trading Standards Branch is at the Department of Commerce, 176 Newtownbreda Road, Belfast BT8 4QS. Personal enquiries may be made at the Companies Registry, Department of Commerce, 43-47 Chichester Street, Belfast BT1 4RJ.

There are six categories of licence and you could need more than one. The cost of a licence for any one category is £45, with an additional fee of £10 for each of any additional categories for which you may require to be licensed. The licences are valid for three years.

Licences are required by the trader himself if he or she is

a sole trader, but by the company in the case of a limited company. In this respect they differ from most other trading licences.

It is not necessary to trade under the name of the licensee – for example a sole trader would have a licence under his or her own name, but might conduct the business under a different, registered business name. In such a case the trading name, however, has to be specified in the licence.

The Office of Fair Trading may reject a trading name which they think to be misleading or undesirable, even if it has been accepted for registration as a business name. They will not normally accept any name that should have been registered under the Registration of Business Names Act of 1916 but which has not in fact been registered.

The Consumer Credit Act is concerned with any form of credit business in which the credit – *not* the total price – is not more than £5,000. Sole traders and partnerships – but *not* limited companies – who only enter into transactions where the credit is £30 or less are excluded, for the time being, from the licensing provisions. (This is the deferment that allows the little corner shop to 'give tick' until the end of the week.)

Most readers of this book who may need a licence, either when they enter self-employment or at some future time, are likely to need either or both Category A and Category C licences. The following brief descriptions, however, are sufficiently detailed to show you whether you may need a licence under any of the six categories.

CATEGORY A LICENCE (CONSUMER CREDIT BUSINESS)

If you lend money, offer credit, or give customers or clients time to pay for goods *or* services – even if this means putting goods aside until they are paid for – you may be carrying on a consumer credit business. The term 'credit' includes hire-purchase, instalment sales, cash loans, overdrafts, budget or subscription accounts, mortgage agreements, credit cards and trading checks. The upper limit of £5,000, and the current lower limit of £30, apply to each separate transaction.

You do not need a licence if you grant credit only to limited companies. You do not need one if you accept someone else's credit cards or trading checks. This means, for example, that you may accept Barclaycard and Access business, and can honour manufacturers' coupon reduction offers without having to be licensed yourself.

You do not need a licence if you let your customers or clients pay their bills *in full* at the end of the week, month, or whatever period you work to.

Examples of Category A licence holders are : retailers or trade suppliers offering credit; pawnbrokers; money lenders; mail order traders; and tallymen.

If you need a licence in this category you will find that there are some exemptions. These are detailed in the booklet 'Regulated and Exempt Agreements', obtainable from the Office of Fair Trading. Of these only one is of possible interest to any reader of this book. This is what is called 'Normal Trade Credit'.

Normal trade credit allows exception if the customer repays the credit for goods or services in *one* lump sum. This allows normal trade or business invoicing and payment after delivery.

The exemption also applies if the credit relates to one particular purchase only and if the customer pays in four instalments or less.

What that means is this : If a customer has a monthly account with a shop in which goods can be bought on credit up to a certain agreed maximum limit, and the customer buys a television set and charges it to the account, then, even if he closes the debt on the account in four monthly payments, the transaction is not exempt. But if he buys the television set as a single, separate purchase and pays for it in four or less payments, then the transaction is exempt.

CATEGORY B LICENCE
(CONSUMER HIRE BUSINESS)
If you hire out, lease or rent goods under transactions which

last for more than three months in which the total amount of the payments comes to not more than £5,000 you may be carrying out a consumer hire business.

You do not need a licence if you hire or rent to limited companies only.

Examples are businesses leasing or hiring out TV sets, cars, caravans, office or factory equipment, vending machines.

CATEGORY C LICENCE
(CREDIT BROKERAGE)

Even if you do not yourself offer credit or hire-purchase, you may arrange it with other people for your customers. This is credit brokerage.

As a shopkeeper, especially if you sell furniture or expensive domestic equipment, it may be essential to offer your customers hire-purchase facilities which you cannot afford to finance yourself. In such cases it is commonplace for the shopkeeper to arrange hire-purchase for the customer with a finance company. A Category C licence is then required by the shopkeeper.

Another example of credit brokerage that requires special note is the case of an estate agent who arranges a mortgage with a building society for a client. The upper limit of £5,000 does not apply in cases of mortgages for house properties.

Examples of Category C licence holders are retailers, estate agents, motor dealers and accountants.

CATEGORY D LICENCE
(DEBT ADJUSTING AND
DEBT COUNSELLING)

If you help people with their debt problems, taking over their debts, negotiating for them, or advising them, you may need a licence.

Examples are accountants, solicitors, mortgage and insurance brokers.

CATEGORY E LICENCE
(DEBT COLLECTING)
You do not need a licence to collect your own debts. Nor do you need one if you act as a debt collector for limited companies only. But if you collect debts arising from credit business or hire agreements for other people, then your business needs licensing.

CATEGORY F LICENCE
(CREDIT REFERENCE AGENCY)
If you collect information about the credit worthiness of people, with a view to giving the information to others, you are regarded as a credit reference agent and your business needs a licence.

However, merely giving references about the credit worthiness of your own customers or clients, based on your own dealings with them, does not make you an agent needing a licence. Nor do you need a licence if you collect information about limited companies only.

QUALIFICATIONS AND PENALTIES
The purpose of the Consumer Credit Act is not merely to register and license traders who are conducting what is defined as consumer credit business, but also to regulate the traders who are allowed to offer credit terms. You have to be reputable to hold a licence.

As the new licensing system has been progressively coming into force, to engage in any category of consumer credit business without a required licence has become a criminal offence, punishable by a fine, imprisonment or both. Moreover any credit or hire agreement made by an unlicensed trader or credit broker cannot be enforced.

It makes sense then, if your self-employment may in any way involve the giving of credit, or the arrangement of hire-purchase, or of renting equipment, that you should check whether or not you need a licence.

It should be borne in mind that if you come under the

'£30 deferments' exclusion limit for small traders and that one day a situation arises in which you wish to advance more than the £30 credit you will not be able to do so until you have actually been granted a licence. And that could take time. The Office of Fair Trading does not 'rubber stamp' its acceptances of applications.

10: Becoming a shopkeeper

For the reader who is proposing to become a shopkeeper there are considerations over and above the practical issues that ultimately mean filling in forms, making returns, registering and obtaining licences. For all other readers the purpose of this book has been achieved. The shopkeeper is in a special category.

A shop is much more than a business enterprise. A shop has – or if it is being newly opened it will soon acquire – a character and personality of its own. A shop has – or will soon establish – a reputation and a tradition. Its founder and successive owners may contribute in greater or lesser degree in these matters, but none will ever completely control or dictate the incorporeal entity of the shop. Remember childhood – some shops have magic.

Since this is largely what this chapter has to attempt to explain in material terms there is no better way of writing it than by telling the story of how John Doe became a shopkeeper – using the device as a convenient way of looking at the kind of problems that have to be considered. And these special problems have nothing to do with forms, or regulations or administrative efficiency.

It is a fact, for example, that a prospering and efficiently run small shop may decline simply because a pedestrian crossing is re-sited. On the other hand, an incompetently managed shop may attract customers for reasons that baffle business efficiency experts but delight the observant psychologist.

FIRST FIND YOUR SHOP

The John Doe story is based on fact, although the name is fictitious and the details have been embellished in order to include a comprehensive 'package' of the special problems and considerations facing those going into business for the first time as shopkeepers.

Every shop, and its possibilities and its problems, is unique. And, of course, that was true in the case of John Doe.

The shopkeeper himself is the first 'ingredient in the mix' to consider. Our John Doe was about forty-five, married, with a daughter of twenty-three and a four-year-old grandson. The daughter had recently become a widow and she and her child were living with John Doe and his wife. John was a craftsman furrier and knew his trade inside out. He had always wanted to be his own boss and the chance finally came when a small legacy boosted his savings into a capital sum that made the ambition possible of achievement.

It was natural that John Doe's first thought was to turn his trained skill and experience to good account. He had always considered opening or acquiring a ready-made manufacturing furrier's business for he had both good contacts and reputation amongst the wholesalers. But the death of his son-in-law had created a new situation for him, one that dictated new decisions. He and his wife now wanted a family involvement in whatever business he went into on his own account. They wanted to involve their daughter actively to provide a needed distraction from her bereavement. And John was conscious of a need to play a more important role in the upbringing of the fatherless grandchild than would have been possible if he was building up a business in workshop premises which would necessarily be a commuter's journey away from home. The first few years would be all graft, with little time for his family. Only a shop was an answer to the personal requirements.

The reasons for choosing to become a shopkeeper strongly

influence the chances of success. These were John Doe's reasons, and they were sound.

Again, it was natural that John Doe's first choice of shop would have been a retail furrier's business. However, apart from the fact that the capital investment would have been high, sole trader furriers' shops are very few and far between; and to open a new shop of this kind involved an element of risk that John Doe's domestic situation did not permit.

Nevertheless, John Doe did begin studying the business advertisements in his particular trade journals. All specialist trades have their own journals. These are listed in *Kelly's Manufacturers and Merchants Directory* which is available at every local public library.

John Doe also contacted several business transfer agents. Realizing the improbability of finding a furrier's business of the kind he wanted, in the general area he and his wife wanted to live, or one being on the market at 'his kind of money', he widened the scope of his requirements to include any general shops which demanded no special experience or knowledge on the part of the retailer.

Business transfer agents are, in the business premises market, what estate agents are in the residential property market. They are commissioned by the vendor, who pays their fees. They are categorized under the heading of 'Business Transfer Agents' and are listed in *Yellow Pages* directories. Like estate agents, their business tends to be local and the *Yellow Pages* directory for the area in which a business is being sought is the one an intending purchaser should consult.

John Doe also studied *Dalton's Weekly* and the *London Weekly Advertiser*, both of which are market places for the selling and buying of general shops of all kinds, particularly in the London and Home Counties area. Finally he kept his eyes open for advertisements in the classified advertisement columns of the evening newspapers and the local weekly papers.

FRANCHISING

Among the possibilities he considered, John Doe looked at the idea of starting a new business of his own under a franchise.

The franchised shop business is one that has developed largely during the past twenty years, although the idea is not in itself new. Originally franchising was a system used by inventors who, having patented their invention, then gave other people a franchise, or licence, to manufacture, sell and generally exploit the invention, paying a royalty or percentage of the profits in return. Similarly owners of registered trade marks may grant other people conditional rights to use the trade mark under what is known as a 'Registered User agreement'.

The franchised shop goes a step further, and offers the intending shopkeeper a compromise between buying a 'ready-made' shop and launching a completely new business from scratch. The shopkeeper does in fact launch a new business, investing his own money – but he has a ready-made, well publicized and advertised name, a product or service with an established reputation and to all intents and purposes he owns a new branch of a nationwide organization.

Well-known franchise business names are Wimpy Bars and Golden Egg restaurants. There are, of course, very many franchises in which the attraction to the shopkeeper is not the advantage of a well-known name but the other practical advantages of the system if he is inexperienced and needs some initial guidance and financial support.

The advantages are:
1. The franchisor provides a blueprint for the setting up of a new shop. He may find, and will certainly give help in selecting the site of the new shop. The premises and their location may well have to have his expert approval.
2. The franchisor will provide basic training and instruction for the shopkeeper, who will nevertheless own his business.
3. The franchisor will deal with any problems of alterations to the premises and will handle any necessary planning permissions.

4. The franchisor will assist in obtaining financial help so that starting up in the new business will need less capital than it otherwise would.
5. The franchisor will involve himself and his organization in getting the new business off to a good start, exploiting the goodwill of the established name and reputation.
6. The franchisor will train staff if the franchisee requires them — and with franchise businesses this consideration often does apply. He will advise and give guidance in connection with the financial and legal responsibilities of an employer towards his staff. Normally people becoming self-employed for the first time do not themselves also become employers at the same time — that role usually comes later, if the business succeeds and expands. In many franchised businesses, however, a staffing situation exists from the beginning and particular requirements will relate to particular businesses. The shopkeeper then becomes involved in the administration of PAYE, deductions for National Insurance, and observation of the provisions of The Shops Act, 1950, as amended, and any Orders there may be by the relevant local authority suspending or varying the regulations.
7. The franchisor will provide, through his central organization, all the fixtures and fittings needed, these very often being standard to all shops within the franchise. He may provide all the stock needed and, because of bulk buying the price is likely to be lower than the franchisee would otherwise pay.
8. The franchisor will provide the services of experts if the franchisee runs into business problems of any kind, at any time. It would obviously be harmful to the franchisor's reputation if a business under his name became run down and failed.
9. The franchisor will normally supply a stream of market research information enabling the franchisee to keep his business up to date and to know about and introduce any new or improved ideas that come along.

For all these services, the franchisee usually pays an initial fee, either on signing the contract or at the date of the opening of the new business. Thereafter he may pay a royalty, or percentage, on his gross sales or he may also have to agree to buy certain services of stock only from the franchisor who will make a profit on the arrangement.

There are many businesses describing themselves as 'franchise consultants', but at the present time there are no legal requirements and there are no required qualifications imposed upon anyone going into business as such a consultant. It is a fact that some consultants are representors of specific franchisors and that the advice they may give cannot, therefore, be regarded as being objective. While many franchisors offer the franchisee 'a good deal', not all do so.

Apart from getting independent advice from the triumvirate of accountant, solicitor and bank manager, anyone going into business on his own account and considering a franchised shop should find out how many individually owned businesses are already within the franchise. He should require the franchisor to provide him with a list of names and addresses of the existing franchisees, and he should make a point of interviewing some of them.

John Doe rejected the idea for himself. He realized that franchising is *not* the easy way to make a success of being a shopkeeper that it is sometimes enticingly represented to be. The one thing that does not come in the franchisor's 'package deal' is any promise of rewards that are not the result of hard work.

Apart from the fact that the franchised shop system was only just getting off the ground when John Doe was making his decisions, he wanted nobody else to have a percentage of the success he was confident he was going to have in business on his own account.

Moreover, by taking a shop with living accommodation and selling his house, he would be in the position that is the best guarantee of success the self-employed may ever have – he would have enough capital behind him to really go it alone.

John Doe gave a lot of thought to the move he was making. He was a man who always looked for a bargain before putting his hand in his pocket. And before long he found the shop he was to buy.

It was a sluttish, uncared-for looking place with the name 'Richard Roe and Son' above the old-fashioned window. It was situated between, in one direction, bus stops on either side of the road and a pedestrian-operated traffic-lights crossing and, in the other direction, the local branch line railway station providing a commuter service to a main London terminus. Beyond the station, the railway bridged the road and here the pavements were elevated and railed off. In short, almost everybody who used the station was channelled into passing the shop.

John Doe recognized a potential little gold-mine when he saw one. He looked no further, but began making cautious yet urgent preliminary enquiries. He found that the original Richard Roe had been dead for many years and that it was the son, himself now elderly, who was running the shop with such help as his wife gave him. They were an unenterprising couple, who had become tired of the family business. They already had an income adequate for their needs from investments and on its own the turnover of the shop would only have produced a meagre living.

John Doe knew that in these circumstances the goodwill of the shop would be undervalued in terms of the potential improvement. Next to good siting this was his major requirement. Together the two things were the guarantee of success.

There was one final factor that compelled his decision. The business was offered with the freehold. John Doe knew that no business is safe unless it owns the freehold, and is not vulnerable to high rental increases when a lease expires.

GOODWILL

If you start from scratch in vacant premises, opening a shop and building up a business, then what you may one day sell as a going concern will include an intangible asset which you yourself would have had to pay dearly for if you bought the same shop as a ready-made, established business with its cash register tinkling from the first moment you opened for business. The intangible asset is, of course, the 'goodwill'.

There are many definitions of goodwill. It has been held to be 'associated with profit and therefore with risk-bearing and uncertainty' and this is quite true. Goodwill has been described as representing 'the general volume of profitable business a shop is doing and the likelihood that it will continue after a change of ownership'. This, too, is a good description. Goodwill has also been described as 'a nebulous concept to which an exact value cannot be attached'.

While this last definition gets very close to the truth, the fact remains that if you are going to buy something, you need to know at least the exact price so that you may then judge the value for yourself. The price being put on the goodwill by the vendor may be worked out, and it should be known and understood by the purchaser.

If you buy a shop as a going concern then you buy :

1. The stock For the purposes of a sale of a business stock is normally valued at current market cost price. Any items of stock that are in any sense shop-soiled, or not saleable at current retailing prices, should either have a suitable and agreed discounted value or be considered as valueless.

The asking price of a retail business often does not include the stock, although this has to be bought by the purchaser. The reason for the exclusion is that the amount and value of the stock is constantly varying. The relevant figure may be finally arrived at when the shop has closed for its last day's trading under the ownership of the vendor. However, a rough and ready valuation may be made by checking and comparing stock at approximate valuation with the vendor's last stock-taking figures. Even so, if you are unfamiliar with the business, it may be worthwhile engaging a professional valuer to value the stock for you. It is worth remembering in this connection that if you have found the shop through a business transfer agent, he is the vendor's agent, not yours.

Should you have any problems in this connection – or, indeed, on any other business matter – the governmental Department of Industry has a nationwide network of Small Firms Centres. These are discussed, and how to contact them is explained, in the section *Where to get Help*. Their headquarters is The Small Firms Division, Department of Industry, Abell House, John Islip Street, London SW1P 4LN (Tel: 01-211 3040).

2. The fittings and fixtures You need and should have an inventory and a valuation, which will be required for Inland Revenue purposes anyway. This a valuation that should be regarded as a negotiable factor, in which case much depends upon how anxious to sell the vendor may betray himself to be and to what degree you may be able to persuade him that you are indecisive about buying. The point to remember is that bought 'in situ', the fittings and fixtures are likely to be more highly priced than if they were discounted for separate sale. You should try to get them for not much more than you might have to pay in a sale room. If you regard them as mostly worthless and ready for the replacement that will be one of your first tasks in giving a run-down business a face-lift, you should say so and negotiate on that basis.

It should also be remembered that the written down value of the fittings as given to the Inland Revenue will assume importance if they are later resold at a higher valuation. In such a case a balancing charge will be made by the Inland Revenue.

Anything you eventually pay for fittings and fixtures above what they are really worth to you in your own estimation is part of the goodwill. Remember that sometimes the vendor has been consistently doing such good business that it has seemed pointless to keep up with modern gadgetry trends. And there are circumstances when the patina of age and usage on solid old mahogany is an asset to be preferred to the gloss of modern laminates.

3. Freehold or leasehold Whichever of these you are acquiring, there are two quite different values for each.

The first value to be considered is the straight market value of the property unrelated to its present usage – that is to say what you would probably have had to pay for it, freehold or leasehold, if the property had been vacant and you were taking it over to begin a brand new business.

The second value is the value being asked for the business with the valuation of stock still to be included but with the valuation for the fittings and fixtures deducted. It will be considerably higher than the first evaluation.

A fairly accurate valuation of the property if it were unoccupied would be best obtained, if you wanted one, from any local estate agent who lists himself in the *Yellow Pages* directory or otherwise advertises himself as a valuer and chartered surveyor.

Goodwill is often based on the average of three years' audited profits, with adjustments made if a spouse's earnings are charged to the account. When you have worked out what the goodwill is really costing you, then you alone must decide whether it is worth it or not.

John Doe based his decision on a little practical detective work, undertaken before he even showed his hand and disclosed that he was interested in the business. Such detective work on the part of a potential buyer is largely common sense, good judgement and good observation.

INVESTIGATING A SHOP'S POTENTIAL

Whatever professional advice may be sought, the decision to buy is always a personal one and has to be a matter of personal judgement.

For example, although the British are spending ten billion pounds a year at the grocer's, 10,000 grocery shops have closed down in the past three years because of the swing from the small shop to the big supermarket with its cut price inducements, quick turnover of perishables and wide range of stock.

In view of these statistics it would clearly be foolish to buy a well-established, highly profitable family grocery business being offered at a very tempting price when, just around the corner in the local high street, demolition for a big redevelopment was taking place and enquiries at the local authority offices revealed that a big new supermarket with direct access to a multi-storey car park was being built for opening in about eighteen months' time.

On the other hand a similar business, with its recognizable opportunities poorly exploited might be a very good bet because the supermarket trend had led to too many small shop closures in the area. This would be true if the area was residential, middle-class and had a high proportion of retired and elderly people who could afford and would not mind slightly higher prices if they bought personal service and a kitchen-door delivery.

There are endless possible considerations about the location of a shop and such is the infinite variety of their permutations, which make every case unique and every judgement an on-the-spot individual one, that John Doe has to be the case-book example.

John Doe already knew that bus stops, pedestrian crossings, pavement barriers and the location of the railway station channelled many people towards the Richard Roe and Son shop.

The first thing he did was to spend a day touring the district. He looked at the kind of residential property from which he could hope to draw trade. He got a large-scale map of the area and marked on it the location of all the railway stations. He measured the distance from each station to the one near the shop. Using half of each distance as a radius measurement for a circle, he described a series of circles with the shop as the centre point. The central area thus enclosed on his map was his 'catchment area' of railway commuters.

Next he had a good look at the shops in the immediate vicinity of the Richard Roe and Son shop. Being near a station this had developed into a small shopping area. He noted that the area had a branch post office, a butcher's shop, a fishmongers, a chemists, a greengrocers, a filling station, a grocers, a newsagents, two pubs, a radio-TV-electrical equipment business, a bakers, a hardware shop, an off-licence, and three branch banks. It was 'all there', and there was also plenty of good, free, side-street parking for cars.

Next he toured the district looking for other similar shopping areas. Then, on his map, he drew a second set of circles, using the other shopping areas, as he had used the railway stations, to give him his radii. Now he had a second, overlapping catchment area for the housewives and other stay-at-home residents. It was looking pretty good to John Doe.

He now paid a visit to the local authority's offices and checked with the Borough Surveyor's department that there were no big redevelopment plans in the offing that could dramatically and probably adversely affect the business in the district generally, and the business of the Richard Roe and Son shop in particular. A new shopping precinct can drain off trade over a very considerable radius. A new traffic or road scheme can cut a swathe as cleanly through the trade of a retail business as it does physically through the locality.

John Doe sensibly satisfied himself that these remote dangers were not even on the distant horizon. He discovered that there were two quite big office complexes and one light industrial manufacturing business in his catchment area, from which the staffs and work forces represented a potential source of custom. He made enquiries and satisfied himself that there was no likelihood of these firms closing down or moving.

Sometimes a small shop draws sufficient business from the employees of one nearby firm to make the difference between success and failure. If that firm goes, the shop may suddenly have its back to the wall, become an unsaleable proposition and presently close down itself.

John Doe also discovered that the town was the nearest shopping-centre for a large camp of American servicemen and their families a few miles away. It did not seem to be a factor of importance because the Americans, who had their PX, did not infiltrate into the area of his interest. Nevertheless he stored this knowledge at the back of his mind, for the Americans had money. They were, in his experience, the original big spenders.

Finally John Doe bought a railway time-table, got up early one morning and spent the whole day observing and making a rough time-related count of the flow of people past the Richard Roe and Son shop.

As he had expected the greatest number of passers by belonged to the two flows of commuters – those going up to business in the morning and the same people returning in the evening. What was particularly interesting to him was that the bus service was erratic, not too frequent and unrelated to the railway time-table. Commuters had to give themselves plenty of time to catch their trains and in consequence there was no mad rush on the part of most of them either to catch their train in the morning, or a bus at night.

The morning stream began soon after 7 am, reached its peak at about 8.30 and had tailed off to a trickle by about 9.15. The Roes did not open their shop until 9 o'clock!

The evening stream began at about 5.30 pm, was at its peak between 6.30 and 7.00, and tailed off at about 7.30 pm. The Roes closed promptly at 6.30 pm.

It had taken John Doe one day to discover that nearly a third of the shop's potential business was being lost because it was not opened during the two peak periods of the day when it was the only shop to cater for the needs that could be stimulated in the commuter flow.

The following day he bought the shop.

When the term goodwill was introduced into the negotiations, John Doe was ready with the devastating answer to the argument that Richard Roe and Son was a long-established trading name that went with the business as the goodwill. He produced a Registry of Business Names' application form RBN/1, filled in and ready for posting.

'This will show my valuation of the goodwill there is to me in the established name', he said to the business transfer agent.

The application was to register the business name of 'The A to Z Shop'.

'We will stock anything and everything the customers ask for', said John Doe. 'Now – can we be a little more realistic about the goodwill valuation?'

And he negotiated the price down quite considerably.

There is a lesson in this for many people entering self-employment and unused to 'market-place haggling'. Every asking price is a ceiling, and should be countered by an offer that is only just sufficiently above 'the ridiculous' to keep negotiations going. The price paid should lie somewhere between those two extremes, but the purchaser will never reduce the price he is being asked to pay unless he comes to terms with the fact that he is now a trader and he is in business to 'drive a hard bargain with no hard feelings' whenever he may.

HOURS OF BUSINESS

The main reason why the shop, as Richard Roe and Son, had been having such an indifferent turnover had been because it had not been open at the right times. One of the main reasons why it was to succeed as The A to Z Shop was because it was now open at those times when it was able to catch an extra fifty per cent of the casual passer-by part of its potential trade.

The Shops Act of 1950 regulates, among other things, the hours of closing and the conditions of Sunday closing. Copies of the Act and Regulations are obtainable from H M Stationery Office, Atlantic House, Holborn Viaduct, London E C 3 (Tel: 01-583 9876). A summary of the principal provisions of the Act, as amended, is published in booklet form for easy layman understanding. John Doe had obtained a copy of this from the Environmental Health Department of the local authority. The local authority may, by order, suspend or vary specified regulations if they see fit – for example, in holiday resorts it is usual for them to suspend 'early closing day' obligations. It had made sense for John to investigate the hours of business regulations with the local authority to check points of this kind.

For example the term 'holiday resort' can apply to a very small district where there are no hotels or boarding houses but there is a single tourist attraction.

Under the Act, with certain exceptions, every shop must be closed for the serving of customers not later than 9 pm on Saturdays and 8 pm on any other day. In a general way the exemptions cover restaurants, canteens, take-away food shops, public houses, refreshment and confectionery sales to members of audiences, late-night chemists, news-stands at main railway stations, service stations for motorists and post office business. The Act is concerned with the hour of *closing*, not with the hour of opening or the total hours of trading.

The weekday closing hours' regulations did not hinder John Doe's intention to open at 7 o'clock in the morning to cater for the earliest commuters and to stay open until 7.30 in the evening to catch the last of them on their return journeys.

The Act also requires that every shop must be closed for the serving of customers not later than 1 pm on one day in every week, the day being fixed by the owner of the shop. Again certain trades and businesses are exempt from the early closing day regulations. They include : retail sale of intoxicating liquors, refreshments, sale of vehicles and accessories to travellers, sale of newspapers and periodicals, sale of meat, fish, milk, cream, bread, confectionery, fruit, vegetables, flowers and other perishables, the sale of tobacco, and the sale of medicines.

The A to Z Shop sold tobacco and smokers' requisites and, since there was no dairy in the district, John Doe found that among the flat-dwelling, late-home commuters there was a healthy demand for bottled milk to be developed. His qualifications for exemption meant that he could net in all the commuter trade six days a week, although he was only entitled to sell these two categories of goods on his early closing day. Sunday opening did not concern him. The shop was not well sited for Sunday trade.

Sunday trading regulations are very specific and detailed about what is allowed to be sold and the regulations cover not only such obvious things as milk, intoxicating liquors, ice cream, tobacco, flowers, medicines, Sunday newspapers and 'corner shop' groceries until 10 am, but the attendance by a barber at a hotel to give a shaving or haircutting service to an infirm resident, and the sale at home of handicraft products, provided the local authority has given a certificate of exemption. In holiday resorts shops may open on Sundays, specified by a local authority order, but not more than eighteen times in a year, for the sale of specific things like souvenirs, bathing goods and photographic requisites.

Any reader proposing to become a shopkeeper and envisaging Sunday opening should contact the Environmental Health Department of the local authority to check the regulations for the particular district.

FAMILY BUSINESS
The A to Z Shop was a family business in the true sense, and in the sense that makes for success. The pattern of family life was dictated by the prior considerations of the business, not the other way round.

The Shops Act of 1950 lays down all the many conditions of employment that have to be observed in the case of shop assistants. However, many of these carry an exclusion clause in the case of 'members of the occupier's family, maintained by him and dwelling in his house'. John Doe was not going to employ anyone other than his wife and daughter.

From the day when they opened for business under the new ownership, no customer on the way to catch a morning train or evening bus ever walked into the shop without finding John Doe, his wife or his daughter smiling a welcome from behind the counter and ready to give the quick, immediate service that meant that neither train nor bus was in danger of being missed.

If a second customer came into the shop while the first was still being served, a second member of the Doe family instantly appeared so that nobody with transport to catch was kept waiting or was tempted to walk out of the shop unserved. The moment there were three customers in the shop during the peak commuter travel periods, all three family members were also in attendance.

The run-down business that had been Richard Roe and Son was rapidly turned into a thriving, prosperous money-making concern and after eighteen months John Doe knew that he had pushed the turnover and profitability to more or less the limit.

During those eighteen months he had spent some time getting to know some of the American servicemen. And he was very sure that the proximity of their camp meant that there was a good business opportunity which was being missed because nobody had been shrewd enough to spot it.

When he recognized what it was, he put The A to Z Shop up for sale. The Capital Gains Tax had not, at this time, been introduced, so there were no complications for his accountant to deal with. He quickly found a buyer, and made a highly profitable sale of the business.

The conditions of the sale naturally precluded him from operating any competitive business in the area, but this did not prevent him starting a completely new business just down the road. He took an empty shop and opened it as a dry-cleaning business.

In his judgement this particular area would not ordinarily have supported a profitable dry-cleaning business, but it was exactly what those big-spending American servicemen were looking for. He bought a small van for a daily collection and delivery service at their camp and within a couple of months the clothes racks in his new shop were always full of service uniforms ready for the daily delivery run.

John Doe had demonstrated already in the district that you needed to get up early to succeed in business. Now he was demonstrating that the second rule for success was to have your eyes open to recognize an opportunity when it was there. Before he left the area he was also to demonstrate another important rule – that you must also have your ear to the ground and recognize when to pull out.

Because gregariousness is one of the main personality assets for any shopkeeper, John Doe had always been a good talker and an even better listener. It was natural therefore that he was the first to hear any rumours being whispered around the American servicemen's camp. After he had been running the dry-cleaning business for about another eighteen months, John Doe put it up for sale, quickly found a buyer for what was a thriving business, and he and his family moved away.

THE SHOPLIFTERS
When John Doe left the district The A to Z Shop was back into a situation where it was providing no more than a meagre living to its new owner. The purchaser had been an administrative executive in a large store. Upon retirement he had decided to invest his savings in a good going concern. That was exactly what John Doe had sold him, but it had needed three people who got up early to turn it into a good going concern, and nothing had changed about that requirement if it was to stay what it had been sold as.

The new owner's wife suffered ill health, and there were only the two of them. The new man could not possibly work the hours or give the service that John Doe, with his wife and daughter, had been able to provide. He opened later and he closed earlier. If he had to deal with a 'rep', or answer the telephone, or go to the toilet then, on most such occasions, the shop had to be left temporarily unattended.

Some intending customers left without waiting for his return to the counter. Others left taking unpaid-for goods with them.

It is of importance to realize that shoplifting is *not* impulsive. The thieves are not mischievous children at one end of the scale and nice but absent-minded little old ladies at the other end. Almost without exception shoplifters leave home with the intention of stealing from shops, in the same way that other people leave to do a day's work.

And nobody is more vulnerable than the novice in the retail trade. When a new shop opens, or an existing business changes hands, every hardened shoplifter in the area descends upon it to see if there is an 'easy mark' – and it is then, in the first two or three weeks of trading, not later, that the problem has to be tackled with vigilance and toughness. If the shoplifters get away with it in the first week or two, they will keep coming back. If the new shopkeeper shows lenience to one of these thieves he will pay dearly for his stupidity.

The average loss to the retail trade from shoplifting is estimated at two per cent of turnover. A small shop, having a turnover of £1,000 a week, is at risk therefore of having £20 worth of goods stolen. And the one-person business, even the husband and wife business, is especially vulnerable.

Light, bright shops with uncluttered counters, giving whoever is behind them a clear view of the entire shop, are a help. Goods that can be easily pocketed should be placed out of reach, for self-service business should be discouraged except in properly equipped and organized self-service stores. Window displays that shut off a view of the interior of the shop from the street are a mistake. So are shop doors that have their glass windows obscured by posters for charitable jumble sales and other notices. The use of big mirrors in the shop, so placed that wherever one looks the whole of the rest of the shop is seen in reflection, are of great value. Most important of all, of course, are the watchful eyes of an alert shopkeeper who never leaves his shop unattended and who demonstrates that he is seeing everything that is going on.

Only one thing deters the shoplifter – being seen.

Today closed circuit TV security systems, as commonly used now by all big stores, are also available for small shops. It is calculated that closed circuit TV can cut shoplifting losses by about eighty per cent. This would mean in practical terms that the £20 a week turnover loss by an average small shopkeeper could be reduced by £16 to £4 a week. Where this kind of loss is being sustained and this kind of saving can be achieved, the cost of the rented system is well worthwhile.

A single camera and monitor-screen costs a rental of £5 a week, but as this rates for tax relief, the true cost is £3 a week.

And shopkeepers using more complex systems and in the high taxation bands gain even higher percentages of relief. Any number of cameras may be used, and linked to any number of monitors. The true value of the system is its deterrent effect so both cameras and monitor-screens should if possible be seen by the potential shoplifter.

A system of this kind, supplied by Videoscan Ltd, 10 Hibel Road, Macclesfield, Cheshire (Tel : Macclesfield 612000), was examined and discussed with a Home Counties newsagent who uses it to give scanning protection to a basement toy department which has to be left unattended for most of the time.

He had never caught a shoplifter with it. To all intents and purposes he didn't have them any more, his two-camera system providing quite dramatic protection.

As for John Doe's dry-cleaning business, the American servicemen's camp closed down less than a year after the business was sold. The new owners had been a young couple who had had a pools win. Well, somebody was going to get their money !

When the Americans left, the business slumped. The young couple sold out at a loss six months later. Thereafter the shop changed hands several times, always at diminishing goodwill valuations, until finally the true level was found for the area and a coin-operated launderette franchise business took over the premises.

Some of those who burnt their fingers in trying to 'hitch their wagons to John Doe's star' might have avoided their disappointments and losses if they had availed themselves of one or other of the many helpful services that exist for the self-employed businessman.

Towards the end of the introductory chapter of this book the reader was invited to take a two-question self-examination to determine his or her personal suitability for the highly competitive life of the self-employed. If at the end of the book the reader's enthusiasm has not become diminished but he or she has recognized that opportunity and responsibility go hand in hand, then there remains one final thing to say. Such a reader will not only enjoy success but he or she will also enjoy the succeeding.

11: Where to get help

This final chapter is largely a directory of organizations and companies whose help or professional services the reader may need or should use. It lists those already given in previous chapters and it adds others that may be of use to individual readers.

In cases of commercial companies offering professional services, the names of such companies are given solely for the convenience of any reader who may experience difficulty in finding a listing of the particular service in available directories. In most such cases there has been personal experience or investigation, but since this has not been possible in every case, these listings should not be regarded as recommendations for which the author accepts responsibility.

It may be useful for the reader to add to the list a personal addendum of those other business names, addresses and telephone numbers of people, organizations and companies he or she uses.

Readers should know the address and telephone number, for instance, of their local Citizens Advice Bureau. Like the local public library this is an excellent but generally under-appreciated service. Certainly contact will be necessary with the local Inland Revenue, Social Security and possibly the Customs and Excise V A T offices.

DEPARTMENT OF INDUSTRY HELP
In the United Kingdom there is roughly one shop to every 112

people. It is often wrongly supposed that it was Napoleon who first said that we were a 'nation of shopkeepers', but the statement is true. It is also true that throughout the present and continuing period of uncontrolled inflation, the self-employed have needed neither unions nor industrial action to increase their personal incomes at a higher rate than wage and salary earners.

It is not unnatural that in a society producing this phenomenon governments should devote considerable attention to the special needs of the self-employed, who may be recognised to be the life-blood of the economic system. One of the most useful sources of help is provided by the Department of Industry. This is the Small Firms Service.

The Small Firms Service was established in 1972 as a kind of advice bureau to which the owners of small businesses could go for help. It operated through a chain of ten regional Small Firms Centres. The present nationwide service has developed widely from this beginning.

The help and advice given spans a wide range of subjects – from sources of supply to Government legislation. The Service makes a claim which is well worth quotation here: 'There is no catch. Our job is to help you to do yours. The small businessman is vital to Britain's economic strength.'

The original aim of the service was to direct the businessman to the appropriate source of information and expertise. Considerable expertise has developed within the Centres since the scheme was launched eight years ago and the experienced staff can now handle a large part of the enquiries themselves, notably those that require information as opposed to counselling advice.

The Service now also has a counselling facility to deal with business problems that are either not readily identifiable in their causes or may require detailed and specialist guidance. In Scotland a Counselling Service is operated through the Scottish Development Agency and in Wales through the Welsh Development Agency.

Counselling is carried out through a network of over 50 Area Counselling Offices by a team of experienced businessmen engaged by the Department. The counsellors provide advice based on their own business experience on the whole range of management problems facing small businesses. They act as advisers and do not seek to take decisions, this being left entirely as a matter for the commercial judgement of the small businessman himself. No attempt is made at providing a full consultancy service and the normal limit imposed is that of ten days' counselling per client in any one year.

The service is confidential and information and the initial counselling session are free. Should lengthy investigation by a counsellor prove necessary, a modest charge is made.

In the first edition of this book addresses were listed separately for the Counselling Service and for the regional Small Firms Centres. However, the Service is fluid, expanding and constantly changing to meet the needs of small businesses, and such listed information is likely to become out-dated and misleading very quickly.

Contact can be made with the nearest Centre from any part of the country by ringing one single number, obtainable through the local telephone operator. Just ask for Freefone 2444, wherever you are, to be connected to your nearest Centre, which will pay for the call.

Written enquiries may be made to:

Small Firms Division, Department of Industry
 Abell House
 John Islip Street
 London S W 1 P 4 L N
 01-211 3040

REGISTRATION

Registry of Business Names

England and Wales :
The Registrar of Business Names
Pembroke House
40-56 City Road
London EC1 2DN
01-253 9393

Scotland :
The Registrar of Business Names
102 George Street
Edinburgh EH2 3DJ
031-225 5774/5

Northern Ireland :
The Department of Commerce
Registry of Business Names
43-47 Chichester Street
Belfast BT1 4RJ
Belfast 34121/4

Companies Registration

England and Wales :
Companies Registration Office
Companies House
Maindy
Cardiff CF4 3UZ
Cardiff 388588

For application forms, personal callers only :

London Search Room (Special Counter)
Ground floor
55-71 City Road
London EC1

Scotland :
Registrar of Business Names
Exchequer Chambers
102 George Street
Edinburgh EH2 3DJ
031-225 5774/5

Northern Ireland :
Registrar of Companies
Department of Commerce
43-47 Chichester Street
Belfast BT1 4RJ
Belfast 34121/4

Company Registration Agents
Jordan and Sons Ltd
Jordan House
47 Brunswick Place
London N1 6EE
01-253 3030

Law Stationers
Oyez Stationery
191/192 Fleet Street
London EC4
01-405 2847

Trade Marks and Patents
Trades Marks Registry
Patents Office
25 Southampton Buildings
Chancery Lane
Holborn
London WC2 1AY
01-405 8721

Trade Marks and Patents Agency
　Forrester Kettley and Co.
　Forrester House
　Bounds Green Road
　London N 11
　01-889 6622/6606

LICENSING
Consumer Credit Licences
　Office of Fair Trading
　Government Buildings
　Bromyard Avenue
　Acton
　London W 3 7 B B
　01-749 9151

　For Consumer Credit licence forms in Northern Ireland :

　Department of Commerce
　Trading Standards Branch
　176 Newtownbreda Road
　Belfast B T 8 4 Q S

VAT
　H M Customs and Excise
　V A T Central Unit
　Alexander House
　21 Victoria Avenue
　Southend-on-Sea
　Essex S S 99 1 A A
　Southend-on-Sea 48944

ACCOUNTANTS
　Association of Certified Accountants
　22 Bedford Square
　London W C 1 B 3 H S
　01-636 2103

Institute of Chartered Accountants in England and Wales
Chartered Accountants Hall
Moorgate Place
London EC2R 6EQ
01-628 7060

INSURANCE

National Insurance; Health and Security
Department of Health and Social Security
Central Office
Newcastle upon Tyne
NE98 1YU
(enquiries initially through local offices, listed in area telephone directory)

Insurance Broker
Wigham Poland Ltd
Bevington House
24/26 Minories
London EC3N 1BY
01-481 0505
(Personal pensions and general insurance)

Shoplifting; Closed TV Rentals
Videoscan Ltd
10 Hibel Road
Macclesfield
Cheshire
Macclesfield 612000

TRAINING

Manpower Services Commission
Training Services Agency
108 High Holborn
London WC1V 7AT
01-836 5400
(Area offices listed in local telephone directories under Training Services Agency. Operates TOPS (Training

Operations Scheme) through government organized Skill Centres; scheme plans to include training of those intending to set up their own businesses following 'retraining'.)

Hotels and Catering
Hotel and Catering Industry Training Board
Ramsey House
Central Square
Wembley
Middlesex HA9 7AP

General
Distributive Industry Training Board
Maclaren House
Talbot Road
Stretford
Manchester
061-872 2494
(free booklets on various trades, including hardware, sports, furniture, books, jewellery, grocery trades)

ASSOCIATIONS
The National Chamber of Trade
Enterprise House
Henley on Thames
Oxon RG9 1TU
(Federation of over 800 local chambers of trade and commerce; able to put you in touch with local chamber of trade)

Scottish Retail Federation
203 Pitt Street
Glasgow G2 7JG
(able to put you in touch with trade associations in Scotland)

The National Union of Small Shopkeepers of Great Britain and Northern Ireland
Westminster Buildings
Theatre Square
Nottingham NG1 6LH
(has membership of 10,500, gives information, holds conferences and meetings, publishes monthly journal, *The Small Shopkeeper*, and issues year-book)

Bee Farmers Association
Mymms House
Gringley-on-the-Hill
Doncaster
Yorks
Wiseton 672

British Chinchilla Breeders Association
Highfield House
24 Curzon Park North
Chester

National Farmers Union
Agriculture House
Knightsbridge
London SW1
01-834 4333

Fur Breeders Association
Beaver Hall
Garlick Hill
London EC4
01-248 9095

National Federation of Wholesale Grocers and Provision Merchants
18 Fleet Street
London EC4
01-353 8894

The National Hairdressers Federation
11 Goldington Road
Bedford
Bedford 53245

National Market Traders Federation
87 Spital Hill
Sheffield

National Federation of Builders and Plumbers Merchants
15 Soho Square
London w 1
01-439 1753

National Federation of Retail Newsagents
3 Bridewell Place
London e c 4
01-252 6816

Index

Accidents, liability insurance, 129
Accountants, 21, 52, 55
Accountancy year, 59
Advertising, businesses for sale, 150
Age, commencement of self-employment, 3–5
  National Insurance limits, 100–2, 116
Age-linked pension tax concessions, 122
Agents, VAT, 111
Annual single-payment pension scheme, 125
Annual returns, 62, 71
Appeals, taxation, 71
Architects, 140
Area development plans, 159
Articles of Association, 28
Assessments, tax inspector's, 62, 71, 74
Audited accounts, 30

Balance sheet, 30, 62
Bank loans, 36–9
Banking services, 35
Block discounting, 44
Boarding houses, 103
Boats, selling, 102
Building construction, tax allowances, 65
  VAT, 102
Burst pipes insurance, 130
Business, commencement date, 14
  expenditure, 65–7
  hours, 161
  names registration, 22
  transfer agents, 150

Capital allowances, 63
  revenue expenditure, 63
Capital Gains Tax, 68
Cars, insurance cover, 129
  tax allowances, 63, 65
  second-hand businesses, 102
Cash book, 81
Catering, 103
Change of use of premises, 137
Clothing, tax allowances, 56, 66
Commuted pension, 127
Company pensions, 126
Company registration, 28–30
Consumer credit licences, 25, 141–7
Contracting-out, 108
Covenants, 138
Customer accounts, 82

Deed of partnership, 27
Deferments, consumer credit limits, 146
  Inland Revenue, 71
  National Insurance contributions, 59, 110, 114
Deposit administration pensions, 125
Depreciation, charges and funds, 41
Development loans, 38, 46
Direct debit payments, 106
Directorships, National Insurance, 108
Double-entry book-keeping, 83–4
Dual purpose expenditure, 66

Early pensions, 123
Earnings, special rule for pensioners, 116

Employees, accident liability, 129
  P A Y E and National Insurance, 62
Endowment policies, 119
Entertainment expenses, 65
Equipment leasing, 44
Exceptions and exemptions, National Insurance, 110, 111, 114
Explosions, insurance, 130
Exporters, 11, 101

Factoring, 42
Farms, insurance, 133
Fees, business names, 23
  company registrations, 29
  consumer credit licences, 142
Filing system, 75
Fire insurances, 130
Fittings and fixtures, 156
Floating loans, 38
Flood insurance, 130
Forms required, business names, 15, 23
  company registration, 29
  consumer credit licences, 142
  Inland Revenue, 15, 57, 58
  licensed premises, 136
  National Insurance, 15, 58, 108, 114
  Planning permission, 140
  V A T, 15, 93
Franchise consultants, 153
Franchising, 151
Fraud insurance, 133
Freeholds, 154, 156
Funding, 40, 41, 80, 117

Garages, insurance, 133
Goods in transit, insurance, 133
Goodwill, 154
Graduated pensions, 108

Hire purchase, business, 44
  consumer credit, 143
Home-based businesses, 6–9, 67
Husband and wife's tax positions, 68, 70, 113
Hotels, 103, 113
Hours of business, 161

Imports and exports, 101
Industrial plant insurance, 133
Innovation capital, 46

Inputs and outputs, V A T, 91, 95–6
Insurance brokers, 48, 121
Invoice book, 79
Invoice discounting services, 43
Invoicing for V A T, 94, 98, 101

Licensed premises, 133, 135
Licences, consumer credit, 26, 141–7
Licences, list of principal trading, 136
Life insurance, pension linked, 123
Lifts, insurance, 130
Loans, banks, 38
  business funds, 40
  innovation capital, 46
  mortgages, 45
  private, 52
Loss of profit insurance, 132

Mail order businesses, 11
Malicious damage insurance, 131
Meals, staff and V A T, 103
Money, insurance against loss, 132
Mortgages, 45

National Insurance, age limits, 100–2, 116
  benefits, 107
  commencement of self-employment, 58
  contracting-out, 108
  contribution classes, 108, 111
  deferments, 59, 110, 114
  direct debit payments, 106
  directorships, 108
  exceptions and exemptions, 110, 111, 114
  graduated pensions, 108
  Inland Revenue deductions, 15, 58
  partnerships, 113
  pensions, 111–12, 114, 115-17
  registration responsibility, 106
  repayment of overpaid pension, 116
  separate husband and wife tax assessments, 115
  share fishermen, 112, 115
  special earnings rule for pensioners, 116
  suspended pensions and interim payments, 116
  widow's benefits, 111

Index

voluntary contributions, 112
Non-profit personal pension schemes, 124

Office of Fair Trading, 26, 142
Overdrafts, 38

Partnerships, Act of 1890, 27
  deed of, 27
  National Insurance, 113
  risks involved, 18, 70
  tax, 70
Patents, 24–5
PAYE, 50, 69
Payment of income tax, 71
Payroll services, 48
Penalties, business names, 23
  consumer credit, 146
  VAT, 93
Personal pension schemes, 118–24
Planning permissions, 139
Private residence, business use of, 6
  tax allowances, 67
Professional indemnity insurance, 133
Profit and loss account, 30, 62
Profits, insurance against loss of, 132
Public liability insurance, 129

Quotations, VAT requirements, 94

Rates, tax allowances, 67
Ready made businesses, 5, 150
Ready-made company registrations, 30
Receipts and payments book-keeping system, 77, 84
Registry of Business Names, 22
Registration, business names, 22–4
  companies, 28
  National Insurance, 106
  VAT, 91
Relevant earnings, personal pension tax relief, 122
Restaurants, VAT, 103
Restricted allowances, 64
Restrictive covenants, 138
Retailers, records for VAT, 98
  special VAT schemes, 100
Retained profits, 41
Revenue expenditure, 63
Rolling liabilities, 41

Schedule D and E taxation, 50
Second-hand goods, VAT, 102
Self-billing, VAT, 95
Separate husband and wife taxation, 70
Share fishermen, 112, 115
Shops, finding and investigating, 150, 159
Shoplifting, 165, 166
Shop window and plate glass insurance, 130
Small Firms Centres, 156, 170
Solicitors, 20, 28
Starting date, new businesses, 14
Stocktaking, 63, 155
Subsidence insurance, 130
Suppliers accounts, 82

Takeaways, VAT, 103
Tax point, VAT, 95
Tax year, choices of date, 59
  opening years' assessments, 60
Technical development capital, 47
Term loans, 38
Theft, insurance, 130, 165
Town and Country Planning Act, 137
Trade associations, 176
Trade credit, 39
Trade journals, 150
Trade mark agencies, 25
Trade marks, 25
Trade name, 22
Trading year, 59
Trading licences, 135–7
Travel agencies, 104
Travel expenses, 66
Television, closed circuit, 166
Typist, home-based, 7, 77–80

Unit linked pension policies, 125
Unrelieved balances, 64

Vehicle leasing, 43
Valuations, fitting and fixtures, 156
  premises, 156
  stock, 155
Value Added Tax, how it works, 87
  quarterly returns, 92
Venture capital, 46

'Wholly and exclusively' tax rule, 66

Wife, employment of, 69
  separate taxation, 70, 113
With-profits pensions schemes,
  119, 120, 124

Women, business names rule, 23
Writing-down allowance, 64

Zero-rated goods, 92, 95